Appearances Are Sometimes a Misleading Masquerade!

SUBTLE SABOTAGE

Overcoming Low Self-Esteem & Chronic Alcoholism, to Caring After a Son with Severe Autism & Celiac Disease, to Conquering Weight Loss & Pain Issues Through Natural & Alternative Methods

LISA HAKES

Copyright © 2019 by Lisa Hakes

All rights reserved.

No part of this book may be reproduced in any form or by any electronic or mechanical means, including information storage and retrieval systems, without written permission from the author, except for the use of brief quotations in a book review.

Cover Created by Cover Design Studio

Edited by Kristen Forbes (deviancepress.com)

Interior design by Kristen Forbes (deviancepress.com)

Disclaimer:

The stories in this book reflect the author's recollection of events. Some names and locations have been changed or omitted to protect the privacy of those depicted. Dialogue has been recreated from memory.

This book is not intended as a substitute for the medical advice of a physician.

I want to thank my family for their love and support. Also, my friends, Debbie and Lynn, for their support in my book, and for their friendship.

CONTENTS

Prologue	1
1. Beginnings	5
2. Hauntingly Dim Memories	17
3. Lost Girl in a Bottle	23
4. Rock Bottom	31
5. Why?	41
6. Sibling Rivalry & Mischief	49
7. Blinded by Love	53
8. Mom's Chaotic Last Years	59
9. Who was Mom, Really?	67
Photos I	73
10. Beliefs	81
11. Moving on and Complex Birthing	89
12. Chemical Destruction	93
13. Runaway Autism Child	99
14. Shattered Immune System	111
15. Celiac and Gastrointestinal Disease	123
16. Emaciated	133
17. Insanity	143
18. My Dynamic Offspring	155
19. Furry Family Members & Seizures	165
Photos II	169
20. Healing Oneself	175
Epilogue	Part 1	187
Epilogue	Part 2	193

PROLOGUE

I want to start my memoir reflecting on my memories and my relationships with my family—particularly my parents. I want to unlock the reason behind my low self-esteem and chronic alcoholism that afflicted me during my youth. I have been sober since February 16th, 1991.

My writing is an unraveling of years of inner turmoil. Why did I become an alcoholic as a teenager? Why didn't my parents express more concern to me about my problem drinking? I begin my memoir with my childhood in a dysfunctional home, and the story of my thirteen years of chronic alcoholism from ages sixteen to twenty-nine years old. When I was growing up, I didn't think I was living in a dysfunctional home; I believed I had superstar parents! I always thought I was the one who was dysfunctional. I suspect most families have some sort of dysfunction, but some have more than others. I believe my early struggles gave me the strength to later go through the challenges of raising a child with severe autism.

The family I've created with my husband, Mike, includes my three wonderful, intelligent children: Erik, Kyle and Krystal. My children have been an incentive to persevere. Not to mention, Mike, who stood by me through all of this. But ultimately, you must keep going for yourself.

After my mother passed, I really started thinking about how limited our time is here on Earth. One day we are just gone. I believe our spirits endure but our physical bodies go back to being part of the Earth. The memories of who we were fade away over time. My parents seemed larger than life to me growing up, and now they are both gone. I want to tell about *my* life. I want to share *my* story. For a very long time, all I wanted to do was keep my life story hidden and a secret. But now I think it would be great if I could be an inspiration to someone grappling with some of the same issues I have lived with.

For years, I have been told by friends that I should write a book about my autistic son, but I didn't have the answers to making him better, and I was uncomfortable with writing a book which recounted our challenges in raising him. We have tried everything under the Sun to improve his quality of life. We take life one day at a time.

There is so much people don't understand about the autism spectrum. A lot of people seem to think autism is like the movie *Rain Man* or the TV show "The Good Doctor." Both portray savant individuals, but most people with autism are not savant. Most are of average intelligence, and learning is difficult for them.

Most physicians consider autism to be a neurological disorder that affects cognitive thinking and sensory processing. It is considered a developmental disorder. There is much more to it. Havoc is going on in their entire bodies! Most have gastrointestinal problems, immune deficiencies, and a dysfunctional detox process.

People with autism are on a spectrum, and they can differ greatly from one another. My son Kyle is low functioning. I do think he's intelligent, but his obsessive-compulsive disorders get in the way of his learning. He cannot read or write. He isn't toilet trained and wears diapers. He is primarily non-verbal, but he can put one or two words together to help with communication.

Kyle cannot speak in sentences and will not communicate in appropriate ways if there is something wrong with him or if he is not feeling well. He can become aggressive in his behavior when this happens because he is frustrated or in pain. Kyle has celiac disease and eosinophilic esophagitis. In addition, he has a very restrictive diet.

Kyle sees a doctor annually, and he has been seen by numerous other doctors throughout the years. However, the only doctor who has recognized Kyle's other ailments besides his autism, has a child with autism himself. This doctor specializes in the biomedical side of autism. Kyle has also been seen by a psychiatrist, and he received Applied Behavioral Analysis treatment when he was little.

In general, I believe most physicians are very well meaning in their intent to help people. I do believe doctors are a necessity in our society when it comes to emergency care and other maladies. We should appreciate and value our physicians.

However, I believe that there are situations where our bodies can heal themselves; it is a lot less invasive to our bodies than medications or surgery. But yes, sometimes surgery may be the only way, and medications can sometimes help certain people—but not my Kyle! He is sensitive to all medications and most supplements due to his digestive diagnoses and his poorly functional detox system. We have tried numerous medications and supplements over the years.

The opinions and interpretations in my book are from my own personal observations and research.

I

BEGINNINGS

I grew up in the Upper Peninsula of Michigan. My family's neighborhood consisted of average middle-class families, where everyone knew each other and—for the most part—enjoyed one another's company. My household consisted of my parents, Phil and Barb, my sister, Terese, who is five years older than me, my brother, Barry, who is four year older than me, and myself, Lisa.

We had an outside dog named Sparky and two cats, Pinto and Missy. For a time, we also had a couple of ducks, Dodo and Daisy. For several months, we had a young raccoon named Sassy. My dad had a friend who was a game warden. The game warden had obtained this young raccoon and didn't know what to do with it because it was so young. He was aware of my dad's camp property, a log cabin in the woods, but someone needed to care for her until she was old enough to be set free in the woods. My family took on this role. We cared for her for one summer at home and one fall season out at the camp.

I had just turned sixteen years old that spring. During the summer months that we had her, I was her primary caretaker, her substitute mother. She slept with me in my bed and loved to pull the rollers out of my hair during the night. She liked to crawl up and down my pant leg. That was a very special summer for me. I still treasure those memories!

By the time fall came around, Sassy was larger and a little more aggressive. She could get a bit nippy and snarl if she didn't want to be bothered. My dad gave me a pair of heavy-duty gloves to handle her with, but it became time to set her free out on our camp property in the woods. For a time, she stayed around the camp property, but I would still worry about her. I had a hard time letting go.

One day, it was pouring rain outside. It probably seems a bit silly to worry about a raccoon being caught in the rain, but I had become accustomed to watching out for her. Plus, I was young and a bit naïve. I had just gotten my driver's license, so I drove out to the property gate, but it was locked. I went home and pleaded with my dad to go to the camp and look for her. He waited until the rain stopped, and then my parents, along with some family friends who had been over, went out to the camp. It was dark, so we had flashlights. Everyone started calling out Sassy's name in the wooded area of our property, but she wasn't coming to us. But when we went back to the cabin, Sassy was sitting right on the front porch. I doubt my dad had been very worried about Sassy being out in the rain, but it was nice of him to appease me by going out there and looking for her.

The last time I saw Sassy, she crawled up and snuggled onto my lap while I was sitting in a chair in the camp. I felt as though she had come to say goodbye to me. I never saw her again. My dad and brother later saw some baby raccoons hanging around the property, and wondered if they could have been Sassy's babies.

She may have stayed around the camp area for a time, but I was informed many years later by my mother, that owners of a neighboring camp had killed her. My dad must have confirmed this. I think I would have preferred to have never known. I liked thinking that she had gone off to have a family of her own. I assume my dad was the one who wanted to keep it a secret from me. I think he didn't want me to feel sad.

Dad loved Sassy too! He watched over her at the camp during the last couple of months that we had her. He learned how to imitate coon chitter sounds. He learned to do it well!

My dad was a veteran of the Korean War. I acquired this information from my father's obituary. It was written by my mother, who is also now deceased, "Phil joined the U.S. Army and served in the Korean War with the Field Artillery Battalion. He was seriously wounded at Heartbreak Ridge and received numerous decorations for his service, including the Purple Heart, United Nations Service Medal, the Korean Service Medal with two bronze stars, the Presidential Unit Citation, the Republic of Korean Presidential Service Ribbon and Meritorious Service Ribbon. Upon being honorable discharged from the Army, he held the rank of sergeant."

Dad was awarded the Purple Heart for the wounds he obtained. He was in a truck that exploded while passing over a grenade. The two other men who were in the truck died. My dad lost a leg, from just below the knee and down, and his other leg was injured. He also lost an eye. He had to wear a wooden leg and a glass eye for the remainder of his life. I remember when I was just a little girl, he would fall asleep in his lounge chair. I used to think he was awake and watching me, because one eye was open.

My parents would put on Halloween parties for our neighbors, friends, and relatives. My dad would sometimes dress up as a pirate. He made a good pirate with his peg leg and patch over his eye!

My father grew up with one older brother and one older sister, my Uncle Albert and Aunt Evelyn. He also had one younger brother, my Uncle Jacob. Both of Dad's brothers had also been in the service. I have many cousins from my father's side of the family. My paternal grandfather had come over to the United States from Sweden. I never met him. He died of a heart attack before I was born. My paternal grandmother's family came from France. They had migrated to Canada, then came to the United States. My grandma lived to be 88 years old.

My dad was athletic in his youth. He enjoyed playing sports and was good at them. He played basketball in high school, and he also enjoyed downhill skiing. He was also a talented gardener and artist. He could draw some fantastic pictures.

My father was a hard worker. He worked hard his entire life. His limitations never stopped him. He had been a lineman in his early years of working at the Wisconsin Electric Power Company. After his military service, he returned as a junior clerk. After working there for nearly thirty years, he had become the supervisor of customer billing and accounting. He had an early retirement because of his medical issues from his war wounds.

At home, Dad did everything and then some by taking care of

the house, yard, and camp property. My dad was a leader. My mother once told me that other men looked up to him.

Dad loved the woods. With the help of some friends and relatives, he built a log cabin out on his forty acres of land in the Upper Peninsula of Michigan. He hunted deer at the camp throughout most of his life. But as he got older, he preferred to put food out for the deer to eat instead. He softened! His temper also softened in his later years.

Dad wasn't perfect, although he strived to be. Both my parents were perfectionists. I think for my dad, it was more of a learned behavior, or maybe somewhat of an obsessive-compulsive disorder. He liked order. My dad was Catholic, and the three of us children were raised Catholic. My dad lived by the "cleanliness is next to godliness" motto. A favorite saying of his was, "The floor should be clean enough to eat off of." I think my parents' perfectionism was sometimes a bit overwhelming for me. It didn't seem rational to me at times.

My dad could be strict. He could sometimes have a temper. I probably had it the easiest being the youngest. More was expected of my older sister and my brother, being the only boy. My dad and sister had, on occasion, nasty yelling brawls. Like Dad, Terese sometimes had a fiery side. This upset him. It was scary listening to them sometimes. Once, I hid under the covers of my bed. My dad was never physically abusive, but sometimes his words could be loud, harsh, and critical. Despite my dad and sister's occasional altercations, they still had a loving bond and a strong sense of loyalty between them.

Dad was just raised a certain way, and he had expectations of how things should be done. He would get upset if I ate on a tray table in the living room in front of the TV; you were supposed to eat at the kitchen table. He also didn't like when I wouldn't make my bed. He once said to me, "No one will ever marry you if you don't make your bed." Well, I still don't make my bed, and it's not a problem in my marriage.

I find making up a bed every day, that no one ever sees, to be a bit silly. You crawl in bed every night and mess it up anyway. I saw on the news once that dust mites like a warm, made-up bed. It makes a good nesting place. A not made-up bed is better for your health. You can find this info on Google.

My dad was a loving father and a good friend and neighbor. He was always willing to help someone who needed it. The gifts he gave people were of himself. His family came first. He would do anything for us. It was my father who took us places, such as the Fourth of July parades and fireworks. He took us to the beach and the county fair. In the winter, he took us ice skating. I honestly don't remember my mother being along for these occasions. My sister and brother may have different memories because they came first, and maybe some things were different before I came along. But that is how I remember it. Mostly I remember my mother dropping us off for our dance and piano lessons. She also took us to our dentist and doctor appointments.

My dad had been a Scout Master. My mother had been a Bluebird leader. She was also involved in the Parent Teacher Association at the schools, where she volunteered. But I feel my mother took these roles for different reasons than my father. My dad always wanted to help others. I think my mother liked the self-recognition she received. All people like to be recognized for what they do, but I believe that may have been more important to her than the service she provided.

One of my fond personal memories of my dad is of the two of us sitting around the Christmas tree. We each picked out an ornament for the other to find on the tree. We would give each other clues about the ornaments, like colors and shapes. There were a lot of different ones to choose from; my mother always put together a beautiful Christmas tree. This was a special memory for me. I enjoyed the attention I received from my father at these times!

Once, I thought I heard footsteps coming from the roof. I thought it was Santa and his reindeer. I looked outside and saw animal footprints in the snow. It was probably from deer going through the yard, and the noise I heard was probably from Dad scraping snow off the roof. But Dad was amused by my thinking it was Santa and his reindeer, and went along with it.

On Christmas Day, I would creep into my parents' bedroom to announce that Santa Claus had been there. My dad would get up early, while my mother usually needed a little more sleep. She was a night owl. Mom liked her late-night, old movies. She would come a little later. I would wake up my siblings too. It was my mother who made sure we always had some nice presents Christmas morning. My dad was more frugal. I learned later though that Dad was the one who wrapped most of our presents.

Another memory I have was when Dad took me to the theater to see Disney's *Sleeping Beauty*. I wanted to see this movie very badly. I usually didn't ask to go to the movies, but I remember pleading to my mom to take me. My mother said she wasn't able to take me. In those days, it was more the mother's role. My dad was a macho man. His taking me to see this girly animated movie was special to me. It may not seem that special, but for me it was. He made me feel like I mattered that day!

Another time, I was a teenager and wanted to go camping. My dad got the trailer ready to go, and the two of us went, just because I wanted to. My dad would play card games with me when we camped. When my family went on a vacation, it usually meant taking the trailer to nearby campgrounds in the Upper Peninsula. I enjoyed playing in the water, canoeing, and campfires.

I especially enjoyed one campground called *Golden Sands*. They had a great recreation room with a ping pong table, pinball machines, and a jukebox. Whenever I hear the song "Sister Golden Hair," it takes me back in time to Golden Sands Campground. That song played on the jukebox frequently. We camped at Golden Sands nearly every year for most of my childhood. In my teenage years, I would bring along a friend.

My two best friends were twins, Mandy and Sandy. Sandy particularly liked going camping with me when we were teenagers. We liked to walk around the lake. One incentive we had to go around the lake was because there was a couple of good-looking brothers who lived with their family on the other side. We had met them at the recreation hall at the campground, but didn't know them very well. I did get a little motorcycle ride from the one that I liked. It was one of my first crushes.

Sandy and I also liked to paddleboat and canoe around the lake. One time, we were out on the lake in the paddleboat past the hour that we were supposed to be back by. It was dark, and I remember a flood of lights being shined on us as we pulled into shore. We got in trouble sometimes, but we weren't drinking alcohol in these early escapades. Another time, Sandy and I hitchhiked to Golden Sands. It was about a one-hour drive. It was a very stupid idea. The two men who picked us up were speeding like crazy. It was a 55-mph speed limit, and they were driving around 80 mph. It was a scary ride. Sandy and I were praying for a safe return home.

I didn't do "rough it" camping. We always had a camper or a trailer for camping. But I just loved being at that campground and wanted to be there. My experiences of camping at Golden Sands made me alive inside!

One special excursion for me was a trip to Mexico City and Acapulco for a school trip with my Spanish class. I was fifteen years old. A classmate of mine and a neighbor also went on the trip. My mother was friends with their mothers, and I believe that's why I was permitted to go. The journey was good for me because I got to see that there was more to the world than what I knew.

My mother grew up in the back woods of the Upper Peninsula. Her family had also lived in Detroit, Michigan for a short time. She was raised a Methodist. Her mother was of Swedish and Finnish descent, and her father was of Norwegian and Scottish descent. When my mother was a teenager, she worked as a waitress in a restaurant. This was where my mom and dad met. My dad was in the military at the time. He hadn't yet acquired his injuries from the war. They began seeing each other. After my father received his injuries from the war, he was medically discharged from the army, and my parents were married shortly after. My mother was just a few days from turning nineteen, and my father was twenty-five.

My mom was an avid long-distance swimmer. She grew up swimming the lakes of the Upper Peninsula. She continued her swimming until she was in her mid-seventies. She had a bad fall around that time and was injured. This affected her health for the rest of her life. Mom passed away at 81 years old.

Mom also had other injuries from her past that caught up with her. She had injuries from a car accident, an exercise class, ice skating, and waterskiing. In her final years, the waterskiing injury resulted in a slipped disc in her neck. The fall she had was the straw that broke the camel's back! She eventually needed a cane, then a walker, to get around. She always wanted to be top notch at whatever she did. She could be a bit of a show off! It took a toll on her body.

My dad had passed away at 73 years old of a heart attack. Shortly before his heart attack, he had been hospitalized for an infection in his leg. But he returned home and seemed fine again. He also had diabetes in his older years, but he seemed to manage that well. I asked Mom why she thought Dad had had a heart attack. Her answer was, "Oh, he was always mixing up his medications."

Up until the time my mother acquired her injuries from her fall, she could swim in a lake for hours at a time. She loved to talk about how she swam with the loons. She was a regular in the water, and the loons began to trust her. She said she even managed to get near their young. Another time while she was out swimming on the lake, one of the loons started to squawk. The clouds were getting darker, and she felt the loon was trying to warn her of an incoming thunderstorm. Mom managed to get out of the water before the storm.

My mother liked to dress stylish when she went out. She liked to wear Clinique cosmetics. She also went to the beauty salon every week to have her hair done. For a time, she worked at a store putting makeup on women. People seemed to be drawn to my mother. Mom had a pleasant personality and a friendly demeanor about her. She was polite and kind to others. This positive outward behavior was a good example for us kids. Looking back, I see how important it was for her to have admirers. I admired my mother as well. Both my parents had good social etiquette.

My mother had good manners. She always stressed saying "thank you" or writing a thank you note for anything given to us. She wanted to be thanked for any gift she gave someone. My dad always stressed being "on time." But my mother was rarely on time. I remember many situations where my dad told my mom to hurry. As an adult, it's important to me to be both on time and to always say thank you. It is the thought that counts, and that is what should be appreciated! My parents probably learned their manners from their own parents.

At my mother's church, she often did the bulletin boards. She had artistic ability. She was very creative in her displays. I always loved how she decorated the house to a tee for every holiday. It was fun, especially at Halloween and Christmas! My mom wanted her home to be beautiful, as well as herself. She made these holidays magical! I have a little of the decorating bug in me as well, but not nearly as much as my mother did. I learned from her, and my siblings did too. They have the decorating bug as well, especially my sister.

When I do my holiday decorating, it makes me feel close to my mother again. It was a side of her that I really liked. I cannot help but feel her essence when I do my decorating.

I also do some summer decorating outside with fairies and potted flowers. I enjoy feeding and watching the birds in the summer. I don't do gardening. Growing up, I wasn't taught how to garden, or much of anything for that matter, including cooking. I learned more about cooking from my husband, Mike, than I did from my mother. Mike learned about cooking from his own mother. I only do basic cooking. I haven't taught my daughter much about cooking because my own cooking is limited. Still, I have learned how to put on a good Thanksgiving dinner. In her later years, my mother gave me a few recipes that I asked for.

My mom always wanted her home to be showy, both inside and out. She wanted every blade of grass to be green! She bought an underground water sprinkler system for her yard in her later years. My dad also liked his yard well kept. He didn't like weeds in the yard. But his perfection was more about everything looking healthy, clean, and tidy. That was important to my mother as well, but she also wanted everything to be attractive and beautiful. I don't think this was a learned behavior for my mother. I don't remember my grandparents ever having extravagant decor in their home.

A lot of people like to look and do their best. People also like their homes to look nice. That is perfectly normal behavior, but it seemed to be the theme of my mother's life. She seemed to do everything on a grandiose level!

2
HAUNTINGLY DIM MEMORIES

How I spent my time growing up, was an indication of my insecurities. I had few friends and I wasn't involved in any activities. However, my sister and I were both in dance classes in our early years growing up. I enjoyed dance. I also took piano lessons. But as my mother put it, I only did it to please her. When the lessons were over, I was done with it.

My mother liked to see her children dressed well, like herself. I liked the clothes and jewelry that she let me pick out to have. I also always had toys. My mother liked to give gifts, and not only to her family, but to anyone she felt a connection to. She was very fond of the movie *A Christmas Carol* where the Scrooge gives out gifts at the end of the movie. Looking back, I see giving gifts as another way she got people to like and admire her.

I have always loved giving toys and clothes to my own children. But I do it because I think it will make them happy, like it did for me. I always loved watching them open their presents at Christmas and on birthdays. Receiving gifts when

I was child was a delight to me. It made me feel loved. At least, so I thought. No gift is greater than the gift of unconditional love. That is the best present I ever gave my own kids. I can see that from the way they are today. Even though they are a little reserved, they have so much more self-confidence than I ever had while growing up. But I'm not perfect in my parenting either. I don't think that anyone is!

I spent most of my time growing up in my room. I felt safer there. But it was hard to find things to do in my room all the time. In my teenage years, I was given a very small black and white TV, but there were only a couple of stations that came in. Usually, there wasn't anything I cared to watch. There weren't any iPads, tablets, or cellphones in those days. I read books, but that could get boring after a while too. I also listened to records sometimes.

I don't remember my mother ever playing games with me. She didn't let me play Scrabble when I asked her. If she ever did play games with me, I must have been very young, as I don't remember. My dad seemed more interested in getting me to play games and do things. I remember him encouraging me to play croquet in the back yard. I enjoyed it.

In my younger years, I spent most of my time playing with my dolls. After I felt I was too old to play with them, I felt a little lost. Using my imagination was how I was accustomed to spending time.

My sister claims that I wrecked some her things. I actually did wreck one of her high school annuals, but not on purpose. I just wore it out from constantly flipping back and forth through the pages. I used the photos of the people in it as substitutes for my dolls. I would use my imagination to create stories as I had done with my dolls. I know that sounds sad, but that is how I survived. It kept me from going insane. I was too insecure to have a real life. It was as if I was creating who I was and what I was about in my imagination.

I felt like something was wrong with me. I even searched in my mother's medical encyclopedias to see if I could find a condition that described how I felt. I found something called *autism*. It described people with social awkwardness. I could relate to that, but it also described these people as having sensory overstimulation problems. I couldn't relate to that at all. I felt the description of autism was much more than what I was experiencing. I decided that it wasn't me. Little did I know, I would have a child myself someday with this condition, much worse than what I was reading about.

I did well with my grades in school until I hit puberty. My hormonal changes and terrible acne didn't help the insecurities I already had. By the time I was sixteen, I started sneaking liquor from my parents' liquor cabinet. My life would then revolve around alcohol for the next thirteen years.

It is hard to write negative things about my mother. I'm still very loyal to her, but I want to get my point across. I have had a recollection of these memories before in the past, but I pushed them out of my mind. I didn't care to think about them or dwell on them. It was if I stored these memories in a closet to forget about them.

One vivid memory I have was when I was only about five years old. I was playing with one of my dolls by myself. I would imagine her tied up in a chair, being told that she was very bad. I also imagined a whip being thrashed around her. But I didn't imagine her getting hit with it. I find it strange, for a small child to be imagining this type of aggression, unless it is based on something.

That memory is clear, but this next one is vague. It is so vague that I'm not even sure if it's real. But I don't know where else this image in my head would have come from, if it were not real. I'm a toddler in a high chair in the kitchen with my mother. She is upset with me and thrashing my dad's belt on the kitchen table. I'm not hit with it, but I feel scared and intimidated.

This next memory, I only remember in fragments. My hand was burned on the stove. I don't remember how it happened. I remember running cold water over my hand at the kitchen sink. I think there was some discussion about taking me to the emergency room, but that didn't happen. I don't think the burn was so bad that it was necessary to go. I think the palm of my had was red, but not blistering.

I remember my dad being angry and yelling at my mom, "Why would she say that if it weren't true?" I believe I accused my mother of burning my hand on the stove. If this was true, I really believe it was an isolated incident of physical abuse. I cannot even say if was true or not. I don't remember my mother causing the burn, and I don't remember myself causing the burn. Children do often burn their hands on stoves. But I wasn't one to make up stories. I believe my dad knew that about me.

One time when we were camping at Golden Sands when I was about ten years old, I came down with the flu. My parents knew the owners well, since we were such regular campers at their campground. The owner suggested to my mother to take me to a clinic in a nearby town. I remember being in this building, but I don't remember anyone being there. It must have been closed because we were there during a weekend. I didn't see a doctor or nurse.

SUBTLE SABOTAGE

I was extremely thirsty. I remember begging my mother for water. I had been asking her for a drink of water all the way there. She didn't want me to have water. I'm not entirely sure why. My guess is that she was afraid I might throw up. But I think we brought something along in the car for that purpose, if need be. I also think she may have resented having to take me into town during our camping trip. In the building, I saw a water bubbler. I asked my mother if I could take a drink. She disapproved, but I took a small sip anyway. I didn't take much because I didn't want her to get upset. I was still very dehydrated.

People are supposed to drink lots of fluids when they have the flu, to keep them from getting dehydrated. I trusted her when she said that I shouldn't have water. When we were nearly back to the campground, Mom finally let me have some water. My guess is that she didn't want me to say to my dad, "She wouldn't let me have water." I said something anyway. My dad said in his boisterous voice, "Give her some water." That is all I can remember. Looking back at this, not giving me water seems a bit cruel. What I remember the most about this incident is not being sick but being so extremely thirsty.

An incident happened when I was twelve years old. I was hungry, and there wasn't much left to eat in the house. I asked my mom to go grocery shopping. We were in the store shopping when I started to not feel well. I told her multiple times that I didn't feel well and asked if I could go wait in the car for her. She finally gave me the keys to the car. I must have been looking flushed by that time. As I walked out through the automatic doors, everything started to go black. I collapsed on the ground in front of the doors outside the store. It was in the parking area, and a car was coming in. He stopped and helped me to our car. He then went into the store and had my mother paged. My mom came running out to the car. She looked flustered and embarrassed. She didn't have the groceries with her. I wonder what the man said to her!

I had a huge, deep scrape on my knee from falling. It took several months for it to heal. This all could have been prevented, if she had just let me go to the car when I first asked.

At the age of twelve, I felt suicidal. I felt very alone and invisible in the world. One time, I took many aspirin as an attempt to kill myself. I didn't take enough. I just ended up with my head feeling very strange. No one ever knew!

3
LOST GIRL IN A BOTTLE

Something wasn't right with me to turn to alcoholism at such an early age. In my youth, as far back as I can remember, I was always self-conscious and insecure. I had low self-esteem. I tended to cling to my mother. I had very few friends because I was so insecure. I did play dolls with a couple of girls in the neighborhood when I was very little. I didn't have many friends at school. As I mentioned earlier, my two closest friends in elementary school through high school were twin sisters. I think I would have been even more lost if it hadn't been for them.

I wasn't into sports or into anything for that matter. I did enjoy singing in my chorus class. Anything having to do with music. But I never succeeded in playing any musical instruments.

When I was sixteen, I started sneaking alcohol from my parents' liquor cabinet. My parents enjoyed social drinking, but neither of them had a drinking problem. Their perfectionism was there priority. It would be hard to be perfect if you were intoxicated all the time. Alcoholism does not run in my family. Treatment programs tell you addiction can be heredity, but in my opinion, addiction is usually comes from a desire to escape from mental anguish or physical pain. Also, a person might grow an addiction from too much partying. Sometimes it may even be learned behavior. Frequent repetition of drinking, or drugs of any kind, can lead to a physical and mental addiction.

I would drink hard liquor before I went to school. This soon led to my overdosing on vodka at an out-of-town public school basketball game. Sandy was with me at the time. I had to go to the hospital to have my stomach pumped. I really don't remember much about it. I was in a blackout through most of it. Blackouts would become a frequent event in my life in the following years. After this occurrence, it was suggested to my parents that I talk with a lady from Alcoholics Anonymous. I believe I spoke with her only one time.

I did some very stupid things during these early drinking years. A lot of it, I don't remember. There was one boy in high school who I had a crush on, who was kind of a bad boy type. After turning eighteen, I had a drunken night at a bar and snuck into his house. He wasn't home. All I remember is being in a bedroom upstairs. His mother came upstairs when she heard something. I crawled under the bed covers. At first, she thought I was her daughter, because she called out her name. But she soon realized that I wasn't her daughter. She was a very nice lady. She handled the situation by finding out who I was, and then she called my parents to come and pick me up. I think she realized that I was no threat. No police were called.

Because I was so embarrassed about this incident, one

escapade led to another. I decided to run away. I packed a few things and snuck out of the house early one summer morning. I hitchhiked to a neighboring town. I found a campground in the area to go to. I slept on the ground at night. One person let me sleep on his lounge chair outside his trailer one night. I was there for several days before I was ready to finally call someone. I was ready to go home. I tried calling the twins on a payphone, but their mother answered. She was a wonderful, dear lady. After speaking to her, I called home next. I made it home.

The twins and I enjoyed crossing the state border over to Wisconsin where the legal drinking age was eighteen at the time. I want to emphasize that neither of the twins ever had a problem with drinking; they were just having fun in their youth. The three of us loved to dance! It was the early 1980s, and disco era was still going. Dance floors and strobe lights in the taverns were popular. Getting on the dance floor was one of the few things that made me feel good about myself. I will always love 1980s music. It is still mostly what I listen to today.

This was in the early years of my alcoholism, and many times I drank too much. One time I wandered off into the woods behind a favorite bar we were at. It was during the cold snowy months of winter. All I was wearing was a light handkerchief dress and high heels. I made it back to the bar, but an ambulance had been called to check me out. Mandy was with me that night. Both Mandy and Sandy experienced some of my self-destructive drinking behavior. As I mentioned earlier, Sandy had been with me at the school basketball game that I overdosed at. I was lucky to have two such loyal friends!

I met my husband at one of these bars. I was eighteen and

Mike was twenty. Mike and his friend asked Sandy and I to dance. I gave Mike my phone number, and we started dating. We were both still going to college, so we only saw each other periodically. We attended different colleges in the Upper Peninsula. We dated for five years before we got married. He had broken off with me once because of my drinking, but we got back together. We got married the summer after I graduated. He had already graduated. Mike also had his first job as a mechanical engineer.

When I started college, I was taking elective courses that were offered in our hometown from Northern Michigan University, where I attended college. My mother was doing the same. She was going back to school in her mid-forties. She had never attended college before. My dad's medical retirement from the service funded our education. I also received an allowance from this funding, so I had money to buy alcohol.

My mother and I both majored in Criminal Justice Corrections. After completing our electives in town, we moved in together in an apartment on campus. We would go home every weekend. My mother and I attended many classes together, both in our hometown and on campus at NMU. I still felt a need to be close to my mother.

When we came home on the weekends, I would go across the border to Wisconsin to buy liquor. I would stuff it into my suitcases every week. I liked Jim Beam and Yukon Jack whiskey. I didn't like vodka anymore after that basketball game! I always insisted on carrying my own luggage to the car whenever we got ready to go back to NMU. I didn't want my dad to know how heavy the suitcases were that were carrying bottles of liquor. When my mom and I got up to

NMU, I would hide them under my mattress. I attended my classes intoxicated most of the time. I'm amazed I passed! I'm sure I would have done much better if I hadn't been drinking.

In our two-bedroom apartment on campus, Mom spent most of her time studying. She was always pleasant towards me, but I felt empty and non-existent in my surroundings. I would try to do some studying in my room, but it was hard to when I was in a drunken state.

I don't know what my mother was thinking at the time. We were in proximity of one another quite often in those days. I don't know how she couldn't have known. I tried to suck on candy and chew gum to hide the smell of alcohol, but I don't really believe it did that good of a job.

The two of us went to the theatre to see a movie, *Ghost Story* starring Fred Astaire, while still attending college classes together in our hometown. I believe it was the only movie I ever went to with my mother. During the movie, I got up to "use the bathroom" and sneak a few swigs of whiskey. I'm sure I chewed some gum afterward. Again, I doubt that would've covered up the smell. I was sitting right next to my mother. Nothing was ever said to me about my drinking.

After my mother passed away, I obtained a lot of her old college assignments. One was a literature assignment about the movie we saw together. My mom wrote about how nice it was for us to go see a movie together, like girlfriends. It was nice to read, but it seems to me that she should have felt very worrisome about the situation. I was on my way to destroying myself. It would seem that my mother chose not to think about what I was doing to myself. I might be able to understand her not knowing exactly what to do, but I cannot understand her lack of communication with me in dealing with the situation.

We were side by side too often while attending classes at NMU for her not to pick up on my drinking. It just didn't seem to be in her, to show me concern.

My dad was back home. When I was at home, I was in my room. My dad had trouble with communicating in a sensitive manner. But even his carrying on was a sign that he cared.

My dad once noticed my alcohol breath when he was driving me to high school one morning, despite my efforts to cover up the smell. I remember there being a great deal of concern about it from him. He was worried!

I don't remember my mom ever sitting down with me and talking to me about my alcohol problem. When I was younger, I don't remember by mother talking to me about any issues I had. I remember once when I was upset about something, and I went crying to my room. I remember hearing my dad saying to my mother, "Go and talk to her." She came to my room. She didn't say much, but I was still very happy about her being there. However, it was my dad's suggestion that she come up. Otherwise, she wouldn't have been there. My dad felt that type of role belonged to the mother.

I was told by a friend of my mother, years later, how Mom had told her friend how worried she had been about me during my heavy drinking years. That is what she told people. But interestingly, she never told me how worried she was about my drinking.

When I was still attending public school, I was bullied regularly by a few select students, especially in gym class. I was lost when the twins were not at school. It was the same way when we went to a relative's home. I could be surrounded by people, but feel alone. I felt like I didn't exist.

When my mother and I were attending NMU, she befriended one of the bullies who had been in my gym class. The bully was majoring in Criminal Justice too. This felt like a betrayal to me. I couldn't understand why she would befriend someone who had tormented me as a youth. This heckler was the sidekick of the main malicious belittler in my gym class.

I went through my first substance abuse program at the hospital in Marquette, MI. This was the city I was attending college in. I didn't do drugs. I knew how to get alcohol. I didn't have any party connections with people, because I wasn't a partier. I was a lone drinker, except for the times I went to the bar with the twins or Mike.

I was in both an outpatient and an inpatient substance abuse program during the time I was attending college. My professors had noticed I had a problem. With my mother and I being in the same classes, we had a lot of the same professors. We also had the same college advisor. He was an attractive man, and I had a big crush on him. He was aware of my crush on him, and he somewhat befriended me. But being my friend during this time took a lot of patience. This professor did have a very pretty and kind wife. She was a counselor. I liked her.

I believe my professor/advisor was the one who talked to my mother about getting me a counselor of my own to talk to on campus. I remember him personally walking with my mother and I over to the counseling office on campus. I did get a counselor, and I liked her very much. This counselor was the one who helped me get into the substance abuse programs. However, this wasn't the end of my drinking. It would still be years before I remained sober. But these years were my first steps toward getting well.

After Mom graduated from NMU, she had a paid job for a while at a women's shelter. Not surprisingly, she graduated magna cum laude. But Mom didn't work at this shelter for too long. My sister told me that mom had quit because the women working there didn't appreciate her ideas. That is what my mother told my sister, but it sounds to me like they didn't acknowledge her ideas, so Mom didn't feel that she had a significant reason to be working there.

I was still attending NMU, and being that I was majoring in Criminal Justice, I did an internship at the Marquette, MI courthouse. I did miscellaneous jobs. I also observed courthouse hearings. The people were very nice there. I started this internship after going through an outpatient substance abuse program in Marquette. I had been in sobriety for approximately eight months, but I eventually began drinking again while doing this internship.

The people at the courthouse I worked under the most were the probation officer and the magistrate. After having been there for a couple of months with no problems, they were very surprised when they realized I had an issue with drinking. I was close to completing the internship by that time, and soon I wouldn't have to face them any longer. My life was once again spiraling out of control. My drinking would lead me into another Substance Abuse Treatment program, a month-long inpatient treatment program this time.

4
ROCK BOTTOM

I graduated in the spring of 1985 with a Bachelor of Science Degree in Criminal Justice Corrections. I married Mike the following August. I was twenty-three years old, and Mike was twenty-five. We had a very lovely wedding. Mike looked very handsome in his tuxedo, and I think that I looked beautiful in my wedding dress too. It had a very long train, and I wore a beautiful, large-brimmed wedding hat. My wedding hat was never found in my mother's home after her passing, but I do have my wedding dress.

We got married in my mother's Methodist church. By this time, I was abandoning my Catholic roots. We had a big reception. A lot of relatives and friends of our families attended our special day. The twins and my sister were my bridesmaids, and Mike had several of his friends stand up for him as his groomsmen. For our honeymoon, we went to Disney World and Sea World in Florida. Plus, a three-day cruise to the Bahamas. It was one of the few times I have ever traveled.

After we were married, Mike and I moved into our first home in 1985. Mike had graduated from Michigan Technological University the year before and already had a job as a mechanical engineer, as I mentioned earlier. I had volunteered at a Rape & Domestic Violence Center during the first years of our marriage. My job was to bring the women to the courthouse to obtain temporary restraining orders against their husbands or boyfriends. I eventually started doing this intoxicated. I stopped volunteering.

We had our first baby, a Shetland Sheepdog ("miniature collie") named Skipper. I started a hobby doing crewel stitching, which is somewhat like embroidery. But I was feeling lost again and started drinking more heavily. I started out drinking beer. But before I knew it, I was drinking twelve packs a day. Then I moved on to the hard liquor again. I was having problems with drinking again.

I had my first pregnancy when I was twenty-four years old. I completely stopped drinking during my pregnancy. I understood how drinking could affect a growing fetus. Our son Erik arrived in 1987. I was twenty-five years old. Erik was everything to me. But sadly, I gradually picked up the drinking habit once again several months after he was born. Again, it started with drinking beer, and then I started drinking liquor again. I still couldn't see how I affected others with my drinking.

When Erik was about one-and-a-half years old, Mike got his job as a mechanical engineer in southeastern Wisconsin. They were laying off at his former job. It was time for us to move. After we moved to Wisconsin, my drinking escalated even more. My drinking was at its peak. I had been drinking heavily on and off for nearly thirteen years. During these first few years that we lived in Wisconsin, I was doing almost nothing but drinking alcohol. I suffered from blackouts regularly. I couldn't remember one day from the next.

I remember once, I was sitting in bed with my eyes wide open and I saw nothing but blackness. This really scared me! I thought I was dying. I was dying a slow death. I threw up every day. I was very bloated looking and gained weight. As you would expect, there were problems in the marriage because of all this. I decided I needed help. I randomly picked a doctor out of the phone book and made an appointment.

He was a very young doctor with good looks. It was the start of a new crush. It would have been hard not to. I suspect this doctor must have had many patients with crushes on him. My drunken behaviors must not have been easy for him to deal with. It takes time for the alcohol to get out of your system. He was patient. I suspect this doctor has done very well in his profession.

This doctor got me into an inpatient substance abuse program at the hospital in the area. My counselor there told her other clients in the group session that I had more of a chronic addiction problem than they did. It was going to kill me if I didn't stop. I already had hepatitis of the liver from alcohol. Sometimes if I bent over suddenly, I could feel my liver stiffen up. I would have to wait a moment for it to unstiffen before I could move again.

These other clients in the program had a hard time believing that I had a serious substance abuse problem. I seemed so much like the girl next door! I didn't do drugs or party.

This counselor also mentioned to me that during my participation in our group sessions, I was very perceptive of the other clients. I appreciated her comment!

After I completed another month-long program, I had yet another counselor as an outpatient. I became very fond of her. It felt very good to talk to someone who was empathetic and objective.

I was sober again, and I was going to Alcoholics Anonymous regularly. I found Alcoholics Anonymous to be beneficial in learning that there were many people who also struggled with addiction. I realized I wasn't alone. But for me, it didn't keep me sober. I know that Alcoholics Anonymous has helped many people stay sober. I would most certainly recommend it to anyone with a drinking problem. But the statistics on its success are not clear, since it is anonymous.

It is a step-by-step process to be in recovery. I eventually stayed sober in my own way. Different strokes for different folks! At that point in time, I stayed sober through AA long enough to lose about eighty pounds. I resumed my drinking shortly after the weight loss.

Mike and I decided to move to Milwaukee County because the rent was cheaper there. But my drinking continued. I remember hiding it from Mike by sneaking small bottles into the house in my winter boots, but I mostly would buy it when he was working. In the house, I would hide it under the mattress like I had back in college. I would also hide it in the pockets of my clothing that were hung up in the closet.

Mike was at his wits' end! He was about to take Erik and leave. I cannot say that I blame him. But this was unbearable to me! I loved Mike, and Erik meant everything in the world to me.

Once when I was in a drunken stupor, Mike and I got into another argument. I took a steak knife and stuck it into my stomach. I didn't see very much blood coming from my abdomen, but I had stuck the knife all the way into myself. Mike brought me to the emergency room. After being sent to emergency surgery to be operated on, I was told I had been bleeding to death internally. But thankfully, I hadn't hit any vital organs!

I was arrested for this. A couple of police officers came to my hospital room. Attempted suicide is illegal in Wisconsin. This came as a big surprise to me! I considered the ordeal to be a cry for help. The authorities said they would drop the charges if I went into a month-long psychiatric treatment program. I cooperated.

During these month-long treatment programs that I was in, Erik would stay two weeks at his maternal grandparents' home and two weeks at his paternal grandparents' home, both in northern Michigan. On a positive note, it was good bonding time for Erik and both sets of grandparents. Mike was particularly touched by his mother when she told him to give me another chance. I was touched as well!

I always did get along well with Mike's family, and vice versa. Mike got along well with my family. My dad always liked that Mike was a "fix it yourself" man like himself.

I don't believe the psychiatric treatment program I was in did me much good, except for giving me the incentive to never have to go through it again. It felt more like a punishment.

One psychologist misconstrued a drawing I had made of my son, Erik. He was only three years old at the time. The psychologist suggested that it was myself that I had drawn, and that I was still wishing I was a child. I wasn't impressed! I suppose a psychiatric treatment center has its place, and that it's beneficial for some people. But I didn't feel like I belonged there. The psychiatrist put me on the antidepressant Prozac for one year, but I never thought it did anything for me. I discontinued it with no problem. The AODA (Alcohol and Other Drug Abuse) Treatment Programs are much better for people with addictions, even if they are not always successful. I also considered the counseling that I received afterward to be beneficial. I do believe that any type of talking it out is good. The psychiatric program didn't do that for me. I would imagine that there are better ones out there. I do believe an addict needs to be treated as a whole person, and not just for their addiction!

The day I harmed myself with the steak knife was February 16th, 1991. My sobriety birthday is February 17th, 1991. My first day of sobriety. I have not had a drink since. I have no desire. It does not make anything better, it only makes things worse. I'm much more sociable without it. I can be silly and have fun just by being me. Alcohol does not make me happy. In my early drinking days, I was drowning out my sorrows and numbing my pain. I mistakenly thought it gave me more self-esteem, which couldn't have been further from the truth.

Mike discontinued drinking during my first years of sobriety to support me, but it wasn't necessary for him to continue refraining from having a drink on occasion anymore. He now keeps beer in the fridge regularly for he and Erik (now an adult) to have a drink on the weekends or after a rough day of work. I could care less now. I don't even think about it being there. I simply don't care anymore about alcohol.

I, eventually, didn't care about anyone else who drank in front of me either, such as my family. But while talking to my mother on the phone one time, she was going on about the different types of alcoholic drinks that she enjoyed. I was thinking to myself, "Why are you telling me this, of all people, about your alcohol preferences?" Sometimes it would seem like she was tempting me!

I had built up a tolerance to drinking alcohol. I had damaged my liver. That is never going to change. **My body is physically addicted to alcohol.** It does not matter how well adjusted I may have become. It does not matter that I don't stuff my feelings anymore. Alcohol is poison to my system, period!

I also used to have some nerve damage from all my drinking years. My left hand and left side of my face tended to want to curl up. I referred to it as my "claw and snarl." It didn't hurt. It just felt awkward. I didn't walk around with a snarling face! They would only curl up if I allowed it. I could control it. Overtime, this improved, and it is now completely gone. It lasted for only a couple of years or so.

It does take a couple of years for the alcohol to get out of your system. Slowly, you start to return to the core of who you really are. Alcoholics can be selfish in their addiction.

To handle stress now, when I'm alone, a good cry can help. It is a good release. During the summertime I enjoy relaxing in a floaty or submerging myself in our above-ground pool. It is small, but much appreciated!

Most importantly, it's very good to talk to someone. I talk to

Mike. I also have some friends I talk to at the YMCA: sometimes with Lynn, sometimes with Debbie. Debbie and I like to get together for an intense game of Scrabble once a week. They have been good friends and have listened to all my rambling about my son with autism. I listen to them and their issues as well. Also, I have a support group that meets once a month with some other mothers of adult children with autism or other disabilities. Our children are all somewhat different from one another, but our situations are similar enough that we can relate to what one another is saying.

I started going to health clubs shortly after the incident with the knife. I have continued to do so all these years. I usually just walked on the treadmill for a half hour, but I'm using the elliptical now as well. I do this Monday through Friday. It is healthy, and it burns off frustration as well as calories. However, I've had weight issues even with regular exercise. Dieting is a struggle for me.

When growing up, I was always on the slim side. I didn't start having weight issues until after my pregnancies, and then during my heavier drinking days. Later, I put on a lot of extra weight during some very stressful years with Kyle. A tub of ice cream was my addiction at that time. More about that later.

Erik was only three-and-a-half years old at the time of the knife incident, and when I quit drinking. When he was about four-and-a-half, he told me that he'd had a bad dream where I turned into a werewolf. This was hard to hear. I knew what it meant. I hadn't been the best mother in his first few years of his life because of my sickness. But I had always loved him with all my heart, and I know he must have felt that. I had done some damage, but it hadn't been intentional. I'm sure I must have acted crazy at times. It was probably very confusing for him. I was the best mother I knew how to be the rest of his growing up.

I do have to say, Erik turned out quite well! He had straight A's throughout his high school and college years. He has had a steady job as an accountant for numerous years now.

5
WHY?

I have tried to understand why my early years led to alcoholism. I knew I had insecurities, but I didn't understand why. I remember in high school doing an oral book report in front of the class on *The Hobbit*. I did quite well. I received a compliment from one of my classmates. It meant a great deal to me. I remember the students looking at me like they were stunned to hear that I had a voice and a personality. I went to the same school with the same people all my life, yet most of these people didn't know me at all. I didn't talk to people. Only to the twins, and just a few others.

I had considered my dad's temper as being the reason for my insecurities, but I had it easier with him than my siblings did. Plus, he always seemed to be looking out for me. That was something I could always feel, even when I was mad at him because of his temper. Underneath the temper, there was an empathic man. It was the same for my siblings.

My sister would say that I sometimes wrecked her things. Both my dad and sister may have occasionally hurt my feelings, but I know deep down my low self-esteem was already set in place. I was sensitive. I think I may have been able to handle their comments or other people's comments better if I had felt better about myself to begin with.

My mother told me that shortly after I was born, she was hospitalized for a skin rash. She always said that when her anxiety and nerves were bad, she would break out in a skin rash all over her body.

I don't have the entire story on this. I believe she said that they put her in isolation. My guess is that they probably didn't know what was causing her rash at first, and that they were afraid she might be contagious.

She told me that during this hospitalization, my siblings went to stay at my maternal grandparents' home. It was about sixty miles away from our house. My siblings had a bond with all our relatives that I really didn't have in our growing up years. During my mother's hospitalization, I was taken care of by one of our neighbors. They were good people. I knew them growing up. During Mom's hospitalization, Dad would pick me up from this neighbor's home after work. I was only a little baby, so I don't remember any of this, but my mother told me about it.

I have wondered if my mother had postpartum depression at this time, but she never told me that she did. Her pregnancy with me was a surprise. I have a feeling that I may not have been the most welcomed child, based on my mother's skin reaction that resulted from her emotions.

What was new in her life that could have triggered it? Me. I must have sensed her anxiety. How could I not? I think I probably sensed rejection.

I think that from a very early age, I may have had almost a Stockholm syndrome relationship with my mother. This is where someone feels affection and positive feelings towards the person who is mistreating you. It is a survival mechanism. The more I sensed rejection, the more I needed her and her approval. I don't believe I suffered from physical abuse. I clung to my mother. I needed validation from her, but I don't think I got it from her.

Stockholm syndrome initially came to my mind because I had always loved my mother so much, but I began to think her treatment towards me wasn't always in my best interest. I asked myself, "Why did I love her so much?" This syndrome seemed to fit. I went to Google and looked up "Stockholm syndrome between parents and their children."

I found a list of articles online and browsed through them. The one that really caught my eye was, "The Place of Stockholm Syndrome in Narcissistic Victim Syndrome," written by Christine Louis de Canonville, a psychotherapist.

In her article, she explains the relationship between children and their parents from the Stockholm perspective. Particularly, for parents with narcissistic behavior. Children have an inborn need to survive emotionally. Being both loved and devalued at the same time is very confusing. I believe my feelings of low self-worth left me conditioned to have a dependence on her. I blindly loved her and thought she was the only one who could really love me. I was too young to recognize her lack of empathy towards me. I internalized that something was wrong with me!

I was so grateful to find this article. It was exactly what I was looking for. It was comforting to me to realize I wasn't crazy for thinking what I was thinking about my relationship between myself and my mother. The idea of my mother being a narcissist had come to me first. Then the idea of Stockholm syndrome. I had already bought a couple of books about narcissism that seemed to describe my situation.

Outwardly, my mother could be very nice and appear very loving. But underneath, I don't know if this was true. She seemed self-entitled. Everything in her life had to be perfect. I wasn't supposed to touch things, and I was made to feel that I didn't do anything right. I think it was more her gestures than her words or tone that made me feel slighted. Body language can say a lot! I think I could intuitively sense her dissatisfaction with me!

I think Terese needed her own validation too, as all children do. But I think my mother's narcissism made her strive for it even more, along with the pressure she got from my dad. I believe she worked extra hard for validation. I just fell flat on my face! We have taken different paths in life, but at the core, I think we are linked.

In my opinion, Terese developed a bit of a hardened personality as a self-coping mechanism. I became lost in the fireworks and developed an inferiority complex.

From my perspective, my mom may have been a stay-at-home mom for much of our growing up, but her physical presence was empty of emotional support.

Most of the time, my mother dealt with me in a pleasant manner. At least on the outside. But underneath, there were subtle messages of disapproval, which made me feel like I wasn't good enough.

I loved my mother, but I believe she may have damaged my

spirit. It also seemed to be intentional. I believe it was just who she was, having a narcissistic personality.

I think all parents probably do some damage to their children's emotional beings on some level. But most times, it is unintentional, and usually the positivity parents bring to their children's lives outweighs the negative.

The opinion I have of my mother is that she was a covert narcissist. A covert narcissist is not apparent, and an overt narcissist is very apparent. There may be varying degrees of negative behaviors with both. My mom's mannerisms were more indirect, while my dad's were more direct. With him, you knew were you stood.

Most people think of overt narcissists when they hear the word narcissist. Overt narcissists seem to think that bragging about themselves will make people admire them. They can be loud, obnoxious, and full of themselves. They tend to be not so likable, because they are boastful. They are irritating to be around.

A covert narcissist is much smarter at getting people to admire them. They can be pillars of the community. (Although, not all pillars of the community are narcissists. There are genuinely well-meaning people out there.) The narcissist will act admirable so that everyone will think and believe they are just that: a wonderful, delightful person! But secretly they crave this attention of being admired. Their terrific behavior is more of a performance. They are conniving in how they think.

Both overt and covert narcissists put themselves before others. They both lack empathy for their fellow men. However, the narcissist can mimic that they have a caring nature. They have learned to show sympathy and empathy if they choose to do so, whether they feel it or not.

How people saw my mother seemed to be important to her. She had a tendency towards perfection in everything she did, but perfectionism is not necessarily a characteristic of narcissism. There are many people who strive towards perfectionism but are not narcissistic.

A lot of people admired my mother. I sensed that growing up. I admired her too! I admired everything about her. She was also soft spoken most of time, which made her easier to approach than my father.

The daughters of covert narcissists may go in different directions. One daughter may be self-destructive, and just can't seem to live up to her mother's expectations. My insecurities led me to a self-destructive path of alcoholism. The other daughter may have more in common with the mother and is taken notice of more by her accomplishments. But she may also have more expectations placed on her than the other daughter. My sister had more expectations placed on her by both my parents. The oldest usually does have more expectations placed on them. In my opinion, Terese seemed to have a need to accomplish and do her best at whatever she did. She seemed to have a need to prove herself. There is nothing wrong with this. This is probably very common with a lot of children, but I think this need for success was especially intense for her. Terese did have higher self-esteem than I did. But I think that she too struggled in her own way.

Terese was closer to our maternal grandparents than I ever was. As I mentioned, she and my brother had stayed with them during my mother's hospitalization. She had received encouragement and admiration from them. She always seemed very close to them. She was closer to all our relatives, family friends, and neighbors.

Sons are another matter. They simply don't have the same type of connection with their mothers as daughters do. They are not perceived in the same manner as a daughter is.

In the case of a narcissistic mother, her daughter might be considered competition, especially where the father is concerned. Narcissistic mothers want the attention and focus on themselves. But as with everything else, a narcissist also likes to show off her children. They are a reflection of herself. I think that is a conflict for a narcissistic mother when raising daughters.

I couldn't help but see the similarities of my sister and I, as described in the book *Will I Ever Be Good Enough (Healing the Daughters of Narcissistic Mothers)*, written by Karyl McBride, PhD. I intertwined her ideas into my writing. They seem to fit my situation!

I learned about covert narcissist behavior from the book *The Covert Passive-Aggressive Narcissist*, written by Debbie Mirza. When I read the description of a covert narcissist, I strongly felt that this was my mother. I linked her ideas into my writing as well. I consider the contribution of both books to be a very important part of my personal revelation of my mother. These were huge eye openers for me! My self-discovery was unfolding at a rate that was both stimulating and liberating!

6
SIBLING RIVALRY & MISCHIEF

In my opinion, my sister has a "take charge" personality. She has leadership qualities. Terese is like my dad in that way.

Terese can also be very charming and a lot of fun. She has an adventurous spirit. Her two sons, David and Jake, have taken after her in that way. Both her boys have turned into nice young men.

I think Terese may have resented that not as much was expected from me by our parents. That seems typical of a relationship between older and younger siblings. Terese had a lot pressure put on her by our parents, but she also reaped rewards that I never did. We may have had some sibling rivalry growing up, but I do love my sister. There were times when she was like a mini mom to me. She looked after me.

Terese did pull one crafty prank on me when we were children. I think she needed to release the tension she was feeling inside, onto me. In her eyes, I probably got away with too much. I remember once when I was about four years old, and she was about nine. She had me put on a blindfold. Then Terese told me she was going to take me somewhere for a surprise. She had her neighborhood friend along with us. They took me to a wooded area in the neighborhood where she had me take off the blindfold. There must have been nearly a dozen neighborhood boys dressed up in scary Halloween costumes. They all ran around me making scary noises. Even though these boys were all young, they were still all bigger and older than me.

I'm guessing my sister's aim was to give me a little scare for fun. It worked. I was terrified. I just sat there and cried. It was a prank. I was never in any kind of danger. No one touched me. They were little boys having their innocent fun with me.

My brother wasn't a part of this. He wasn't there. When I mentioned this incident to him as an adult, he didn't know anything about it. When I mentioned this incident to my mother as an adult, she didn't answer me. I noticed that she seemed to roll her eyes. I didn't know what to make of it.

Terese claims that I wrecked a lot of her things. I suspect that most of the time, I did it because I was young and careless. But who knows, maybe I did have some sibling rivalry in me too and did some things on purpose!

My brother, Barry, and I didn't have that rivalry between us. If there ever was any, it was miniscule. I love my brother. In my opinion, my brother has a laid-back personality, but he is also a very hard worker, like my dad was.

Being the only boy, Barry had more pressure from my dad growing up. However, Barry had male bonding with Dad that we girls didn't have. He was close to my dad.

My brother was always good to me growing up. He did like to tickle me sometimes, but it was all in good fun! But Barry was four years older than me, and we really didn't spend that much time together.

My brother had one story about my mom that he told me after she had passed away. He told me that when he and my sister were small children, they got into my mother's makeup. They had wanted to dress up like Native Americans and used her makeup to paint their faces. That didn't go well with Mom. This incident seems to be something Barry didn't forget, a time when he really got to witness mom's fury! Barry said they were so scared that they hid behind a headboard of a bed.

I can understand Mom being somewhat upset about the waste of her makeup. Makeup does cost money. But something tells me, she went off the deep end about it. When my brother told me about this, my first reaction was to laugh, but Barry wasn't laughing. I thought it was cute. However, I don't think Mom saw it that way.

After my mother's death, I asked her brother, my Uncle James, if he and mom ever had any sibling rivalry. He shared something with me that Mom used to do when they were small children. My mother, being the oldest, would pick up her youngest brother, Dan. He was just a baby or toddler at the time. Then she would throw him at Uncle James. I have tried to envision this. It seems a little aggressive to me. But whatever sibling rivalry they ever had, seemed non-existent later. My mother always seemed very close to all her brothers. Her parents (my grandparents) instilled in her a strong sense of family. This included mom's relations with other relatives as well.

7
BLINDED BY LOVE

At the time of my mother's death, I still saw her as nothing but an angel as I spoke about her at her funeral. I said, "She was beautiful inside and out." I also commented, "You could just see in her face what a caring and kind person she was." I related that she was always there for everyone.

No one had asked me to speak at the funeral. I simply did it because I sincerely loved her, and it was something I wanted to do for her. When I was told she had passed away, I cried hard. I really do miss her! I sometimes still weep for her and my dad.

I sent mom flowers during her final days in the hospital. The message I sent read, "Mom/Grandma, A True Angel & Beacon of Light! Thank you for being so special! Praying that you heal! Love, Lisa, Mike, Erik, Kyle & Krystal."

I'm very glad that I said nothing but positive and wonderful things about Mom at her funeral service. Any negative memories of her were still buried and repressed. But I now need to acknowledge these repressed emotions. I need to release the pain that I have carried for most of my life, the anguish that no one seemed to know about. I think it is confusing to people as to why I became an alcoholic, and it was confusing to me!

Despite any negative impact she may have had on me in my early years, I really did feel very close to her in the later years. After many years of sobriety, my mother and I became very close friends and talked on the phone. We would talk for hours, every week. I lived a few hours away by car in southeastern Wisconsin, so I seldom saw her. She seemed to like having someone to talk to. She would listen to me vent about Kyle, or whatever. I don't know how much empathy she really felt, but at least she listened to me. Mom also did a lot of venting about whatever was on her mind. During our phone calls, I felt that I was getting emotional support from her. She had become a friend!

Sometimes we would just talk about trivial things or about something fun or pleasant that one of us had done. It was all very nice! She seemed to be proud of me at this time. I didn't perceive that she had much pride in me while I was growing up. This friendship on the phone we had in later years is something I will always treasure and be very grateful for!

When I would visit mom and see her face to face, I would seem to become her daughter again, instead of a friend. It felt like there was something amiss in our relationship that I couldn't pinpoint at these times. I seemed to enjoy the "friendship mom" on the phone more than seeing the "in-person mom." But I still took pleasure in visiting with her.

Mom knew I loved her, and she welcomed those phone calls from me. She knew I was an admirer and that I trusted her. We always ended our phone calls with an "I love you."

However, my mother did sometimes say some things that were disconcerting to me. There were times when she told me her opinions about other people, opinions that I was surprised to hear! Mom seemed to target certain people to ostracize:

When I was growing up, there was a lady who lived in the neighborhood that my mother convinced me was pure evil. I thought she was a witch, and I stayed away. In later years, I found out the woman was bipolar and had been on medication.

Another was a relative on my father's side. She was a bit uncouth in her behavior—not like my mother. I remember the relatives getting together to cackle about her. Mom seemed to be the ring leader.

Mom gave her brother's wife, Betty, a particularly hard time as well, especially before they got married. Betty said to me shortly before my Uncle Graham passed away from cancer that she wasn't going to have anything to do with our family anymore after he was gone. Even though she and my mother had learned to get along, she still seemed bitter about whatever transpired many years ago. However, Betty still maintains contact with my brother, Barry, and his wife.

My mother could say nasty things about some people when she wanted to. Some of these people had some issues that my mother seemed to have little or no empathy for.

On one of our phone conversations, she accused someone she

knew of killing off her disabled sister to get her money. It was money given to the disabled sister by their parents, to take care of her after they passed away. Mom would tell me that this person probably put poison in her sister's food. She told me this more than once. She really seemed to believe it. This disabled person was dying of cancer at the time. She did, eventually, die of cancer.

My mom also accused my paternal grandmother of killing off my paternal grandfather. She hadn't been too fond of her. Mom tried to convince me that she wasn't a good person either, but I only remember my paternal grandmother as always being very kind and nice to me.

As stated earlier, my grandpa died of a heart attack before I was born. My dad always felt his father had had a heart attack because he consumed a lot of salt in his diet. I brought that up to my mom when she accused my grandma of getting rid of grandpa.

She said that my grandma probably purposely mixed up grandpa's medications, and it caused his heart attack!

As I mentioned earlier, when I asked Mom about my own dad's heart attack, she said he was always mixing up his medications. She implied his heart attack was because of his mixing up of his medications.

My dad had his heart attack during the night. It was typical of my mother to stay up late and watch TV in the living room until she fell asleep. She usually didn't go to bed until the middle of night at two, three, or four o'clock in the morning. But this night, she didn't go to bed at all. She slept the whole night in the living room.

My brother told me what had happened that following morning. Barry had called to talk to my dad, and the phone ringing woke up my mom. She went to go get my dad in the bedroom and discovered that he'd had the heart attack, and she called an ambulance to take him to the hospital. Barry got to their house as fast as he could.

Apparently, my dad had been sick to his stomach during his heart attack. My sister said that she had a lot of cleaning up to do. I don't know why my mother didn't realize what was happening in the other room. She may have been asleep at the time. It is also true that she was hard of hearing in the last few years of her life. However, I don't know how well her hearing was at the time of dad's death fifteen years earlier. I don't know why she decided not to go to bed that night.

My dad lived for several more hours after his heart attack. My sister called and told me about our dad's dire situation. It would have been a four-hour drive for me to get there. Mike was at work. Erik was fourteen years old at the time and in school. I was at home with Kyle, six years old, and Krystal, who was about to turn two in a couple of days.

A woman who came to our home to work with Kyle was over at the time. She and Kyle came out of his room, and I was crying.

I always felt bad because I didn't get to go to the hospital to say goodbye. Everyone else was there. My sister did hold the phone up to my dad's ear so I could say, "I love you," but he was unconscious. He died very shortly after. My sister later told me that the clergy person that was present said, "That was what he was waiting for." I did love my dad very much!

I don't believe the accusation my mother made against the person who had a sibling with a disability, or the accusation about my grandmother, to be at all true. I'm sure they are not. But Mom did have a way of making you wonder. Back then, I was in the habit of trusting much of what she said to me. It does make me curious about my mother's perception of things and what she might be capable of herself!

8
MOM'S CHAOTIC LAST YEARS

Mom went on a trip to Hawaii about two years after my father passed. She really did deserve to do a little traveling. She had been to Sweden with her brother in the past, but she really hadn't done much traveling. She went with her friend Ann to Hawaii. They had a wonderful time. Mom liked to brag about how some of the men flirted with her on the trip. She had lost a lot of weight after my dad passed. She looked very pretty. But then, Mom always made herself look attractive. I'm sure the flirtations were flattering and made her feel young again. Nothing is wrong with that. But Mom also bragged about it in front of my Aunt Evelyn (my dad's sister). I didn't feel that was appropriate. My mother later mentioned to me that she wasn't receiving Christmas cards from Aunt Evelyn any longer.

I'm glad she was able to do something special before she had her bad fall, because her life was never the same after that. Her relationship with my sister was never quite the same either, but that relationship also started changing after my dad died and my mom found a new significant other. Mom needed a lot of help around the house to keep up her perfect home. There was a nice-looking handyman named Joe who worked around the neighborhood. This neighborhood was a different one from the one I grew up in. My parents had moved to a nicer house shortly after I got married.

When my mom would talk about Joe, she acted like a school girl with a crush! He was significantly younger than my mother, by approximately thirty years! Mom was a cougar! In the beginning of their relationship, Joe got a lot of flak from people about this and broke it off with my mother. But my mom pursued him. She got him back.

They were a couple for a little over ten years. They never married and kept their separate homes. Joe did everything for her, from painting her home, household chores, yard work, extensive decorating, etc.

Joe was a hard worker. He was high in demand. Joe also helped Mike and Erik put a new roof on our house. We paid him for his services, as did my mother for her bigger projects.

At first there was skepticism from the family, as you would expect with the huge age difference between Mom and Joe. But the family all became fond of Joe. This included myself, my husband and kids, my brother and his wife, plus my mother's three brothers and other relatives as well.

We were all happy that someone was making Mom happy and taking care of her. It was a give-and-take relationship. Initially, Joe had been more of a private person. With my mother's influence, that began to change. My mom and Joe were companions. They enjoyed doing things together. I have no doubt that Joe genuinely loved her. I know my mother also had legitimate feelings of love for him, too.

There weren't any money problems or children to raise in their relationship. It was a different type of union from what my mom shared with my dad. No one could replace what my mom and dad had shared for nearly forty-eight years. No one could replace my dad! Joe was a friend to the family. After he and my mother had been together for some years, he felt like family to us as well.

My sister tried to accept Joe too, but I think her skepticism ran a little deeper. My sister and her boyfriend, Sheldon, had lived together for approximately twenty years or more. My mom hadn't cared for Sheldon, and it created a rift between her and my sister.

Usually you try to get along the best you can for your loved ones, but after Dad died, Mom banned Sheldon from her home. He and Joe didn't get along well either. There are many people in this world who don't get along. People's personalities can sometimes conflict with one another. I think this discord led my sister to not trust Joe.

Mom changed the locks on her house and at the camp property. Mom had a right to her privacy, but both Terese and I have wondered if there may have been something else that she was worried about being found out about, such as her finances.

Having Sheldon banned from the house really upset Terese. He had visited my parents' house for years when my father was still alive, and he has always been pleasant to everyone in my family. He gets along well with my husband. They have football and politics in common. We don't have a problem with him. I think my dad tried to get along with him too. They were both veterans.

Terese and Sheldon eventually moved into a new home and got married.

My mom and my sister were hiking together the day my mother had her bad fall. Mom apparently tripped on a root that was coming out of the ground. According to my sister, they weren't even walking at the time, they were just standing around talking. Going hiking was something Terese always liked to do. It isn't surprising to me that she would want to do this. Mom was in her mid-seventies, but she looked very good. To look at her, you wouldn't have known how fragile she was. But her past injuries were starting to catch up with her. I cannot remember all the injuries Mom sustained from the fall, but it was a bit extensive. I remember her talking about her shoulder, hips, and knee. However, her shoulder injury was more from the water skiing in her youth. I know she would later go in for cortisone shots for the pain of these ailments.

After the fall, Mom also increased her aspirin intake to help control the pain. She always had taken a lot of aspirin, but now the amount she was taking was over the top. Mom didn't sound good in the last conversation I had with her on the phone, shortly before she was taken to the hospital. She was doing a lot of complaining. Her tone of voice was saddening, which wasn't typical of her. She was complaining about Joe because he hadn't fixed her shed. He had been very busy working for his customers. Also, she wanted her and Joe to go to Mackinac Island for a little vacation. I felt bad for her because she was always stuck in the house. I started looking on Amazon for a self-motorized wheel chair. It was very hard for her to do much walking by this time. She leaned on Joe for support when walking or used the attractive cane or walker that I bought her. Soon after this phone call, I was told she had been taken to the hospital. Mom was being hospitalized because of an ulcer which had perforated her stomach lining. Apparently, the hole was extensive. She had to completely go off the aspirin. Joe had to find and get rid of what she had left in her house.

Terese was very attentive to Mom during this hospitalization. I appreciated that because I couldn't be there for her, living so far away. My daughter and I went up to see Mom during this hospitalization, but I had my son with autism to get back to.

After a couple of months, Mom finally returned home. My mother's brother, Uncle James, stayed with her for about a month or so. I very much appreciated his efforts. Joe was around as well, but he had to be gone much of the time to work on his jobs. My brother was also working a heavy schedule at work. His wife, Lydia, would bring food over to Mom's house for her to eat.

The second time Mom was hospitalized, was only about six months after the first time. For this hospitalization, she was brought to Green Bay. The disc in her neck had slipped. That was the injury from her waterskiing in her youth. Mom could barely move her arms or legs. It was only a matter of time before she passed away. She died of cardiac arrest.

I believe Mom's extreme physical pain in her last years of life caused her narcissistic behaviors to emerge even more. Mom seemed to blame others. She told me she blamed Dad for her waterskiing injuries when she was in her youth because he was showing off while driving the boat. This was also when she first hurt her shoulder. She probably should have told Dad it was bit rough for her. I think she may have been the one who was showing off.

Mom was sorry for going along on that walk with my sister. She told me she had wanted to just take a stroll around the city park. But I don't believe she related that to my sister. But Mom could have just as easily tripped on something there, as well!

In my opinion, Mom was of sound mind until the day she died. She knew what she was doing. I doubt she knew how physically fragile she was, but she knew she had some aches and pains. Despite Mom being in her mid-seventies, you wouldn't have guessed how vulnerable she was. She was still swimming around the lake at that time, and she looked great!

I wouldn't blame my own daughter, if I happened to fall on a walk. Although if I weren't up to it, I would tell her. Terese received some flak from others about that day, particularly from Mom! Mom didn't talk directly to Terese about it, as far as I know. But Mom was talking to everyone else about that day.

Shortly after my mother's passing, my thoughts of my sister were strained, because of how my mother had been talking about her. Given our bit of sibling rivalry growing up and my mother's strident words about her, this influenced my thoughts. Not to mention, it was a very emotional time. I cannot speak for other family members, but I would suspect that they were feeling the same way. I'm sure Terese could feel the negative energy that was going around!

It was a disturbing time, and it all felt so crazy! It took some time and reflection before I felt like I was seeing the big picture! I'm sorry I felt friction with my sister. In my opinion, Terese was treated unfairly by the family!

Unfortunately, I have found myself stuck in the middle of my siblings. I don't want to be angry with anyone, including my mother. I just want to take off my blinders!

The more extensive my mom's injuries became during her last days, the more it seemed that her trust in others was wavering. There is no way Terese could have predicted that Mom would fall that day, or predict the injuries she would sustain, or everything that was to happen to Mom in the coming years. Terese didn't know that Mom's past ailments were catching up to her. I believe my mother's fear about her end of days was bringing her narcissism to a peak.

Terese just wanted to go for a hike that day. As far as she could see, Mom seemed up for the task. Mom didn't seem able to look at how her own actions in the past (previous injuries) and present (her decisions) affected her own demise. She seemed to need to blame someone else.

Terese has told me that she felt she had lost our mother years before she died. It all seemed to have started with their conflicts with their boyfriends, and after Mom's fall. In Mom's narcissistic mind, she had reason to aim her frustrations onto her first-born beloved child. I know it was saddening for Terese. She had been very close to Mom growing up. They did things together. Mom taught her things. Mom had been very protective of her.

I didn't feel that same closeness with Mom in my early years. What I felt for Mom then was different. I had looked to her more for security. I was dependent upon her.

However, I felt closer to Mom in later years, mostly because of our phone calls with one another. She was there for me, and I was there for her, during these phone calls. Plus, I felt closer to her in later years because of the bond she had with my children.

I believe Terese was very confused by what was happening with her relationship with our mother. She told me she had gone into a restaurant where Mom, Joe, and her brothers with their wives were having dinner. Terese said she hadn't felt welcome, that she had gotten the cold shoulder from everyone. It wasn't her imagination. I heard about the dinner from my mother's perspective. They did give her the cold shoulder!

In my opinion, my sister couldn't understand how this could be coming from the mother who had catered to her and loved her all her years growing up. She could only rationalize that someone was influencing her. In her eyes, this person must have been Joe, Mom's significant other. But my mother wasn't easily influenced, and she was of sound mind, despite her body starting to fail her.

I believe mom's narcissistic personality required those in her life to put her up on a pedestal. If you didn't, you paid the price. I admired my mother until the day she died, and I'm sure she could sense that. But I don't think that anyone really knew my mother. My dad had probably come the closest!

9

WHO WAS MOM, REALLY?

Underneath the surface, I don't think most people really knew who my mother was. My dad was married to her for nearly forty-eight years, and I don't think he knew who she really was until shortly before he died. He probably saw some signs of her true narcissistic self, but ignored them as I had. It was easy to do when you loved her so much, and she was so wonderful most of the time!

On one of the last phone calls I had with Dad before he died, he said to me, "Your mother, she is not as she seems." He said this in a very serious tone of voice. I felt like he was trying to warn me about something. I asked him if Mom was sick or not feeling well. He said no, that she wasn't sick.

He then said it again, "Your mother, she is not as she seems."

I said, "What do you mean?" But then my mom came on the phone. Her tone of voice was agitated and rough sounding. It wasn't her usual tone of voice. I asked her if she was feeling okay. She said she was fine, and that she wasn't sick. I didn't think about this conversation again until almost fifteen years later, after my mother died. My father died not long after that conversation.

After my mother passed, my brother learned that my dad's Uncle Tom had left my parents a million dollars after he passed away! The three of us children had never known this. We knew Mom had received an inheritance, but we didn't know it was that much. I felt rattled after receiving this information and started going down memory lane. What my dad said to me that day many years ago came flooding back to me.

Given that my father had already passed away, the money all went to my mother. My mother told me that both of my parents' names were listed in the will. She gloated about that to me during a phone conversation. She said that none of the other spouses of any other nephews or nieces were listed in his will. She also told me that she expressed to Uncle Tom that she would spend it all if it were her money. I suspect he hadn't taken her seriously, being the frugal man he was. But she came close to spending it all. My mother also received a substantial amount of money and a red corvette from her half-sister's family when they passed away.

But after Mom passed away, the money was nearly gone. What my siblings and I couldn't understand was, where did all the money from the inheritance go? My sister and I have wondered if she lost some of it on the stock market. My mom did travel a little, but not that much. She bought a new car and did a lot to fix up her home, especially the year just before she died. She enjoyed giving out gifts to people. She was always willing to give a gift to anyone for all occasions. My own family included.

I'll give credit where credit is due. My mother gave out

generous cash gifts for Christmas and everyone's (my siblings' families too) birthdays.

She gave my oldest son, Erik, a couple thousand dollars a year for his college tuition until he received his bachelor's degree. She gave Kyle, my son with autism, money for summer camp for a few years. She also gave my daughter Krystal money for her dance classes for about seven years. My mother loved to go to her dance recitals. She was her only granddaughter! My mother was a fantastic grandmother, and not just because of the gifts. She was good to her grandchildren, including my sister's two boys. She relished in her role as grandma! I would imagine being a good grandmother is easier than being a good mother. You don't have the grandkids 24/7 like you do your own children. She only saw my children about four or five times a year because we lived a distance away.

Something else my mother wanted to spend a significant amount of money on was an underground pool in her backyard. It had become too hard for her to go the lake to swim anymore because of injuries, and the cold water bothered some arthritis that she had. She then seriously considered having a pool built. However, she discovered it to be quite costly and decided not to go through with her plans. But she frequently talked to me on the phone about this pool she wanted, almost as if she wanted me to know she was planning on spending as much of her money as she could before she died. But in the end, it was her money to do with whatever she wanted!

I believe if my father had seen that money, he would have insisted that some of it be left to all his children in his will. I'm sure he would have wanted to spend some of it. Particularly, on a nice new truck! Probably other things as well. But like his Uncle Tom, I think he would have been too frugal to spend most of it. Yes, my mother did leave us money in her trust. It mostly came from the liquidation of her home and the camp property. But had she not passed, I'm sure she would have spent all of it. She was considering selling the camp property for money. She had also talked about selling her house and going in together with Joe to get a home together, possibly on the camp property or on Joe's property.

I have wondered if on the day that my dad said, "<u>Your mother, she is not as she seems</u>," my mom and dad had been arguing about what they wanted to do with the money when they received it. Before he died, Uncle Tom told them about the inheritance they would receive from him. My parents knew they would be receiving a substantial amount of money. They probably also speculated that it wouldn't be too much longer before they had the money, because Uncle Tom was in his nineties. But my Uncle Tom didn't die until about a year after my dad's death. My dad never saw the money!

My speculation of them arguing about what they wanted to do with money could be partially right, but I think there was more to it. My mother wanting to spend money wouldn't have been any surprise to my dad. He already knew that she liked to spend money. There was something more to it, about the "<u>Your mother, she is not as she seems.</u>"

With the echoing of these words in my head, I felt like my world had been shaken up. I started looking back on my childhood. I started pulling up old memories I had chosen not think about. I started wondering again why I'd had such terrible problems with low self-esteem and chronic alcoholism in my youth. I really hadn't thought about those issues for a very long time. It was my secret past, done and over with as far as I was concerned. I blocked it out for years. But now I was starting to remember the pain of it all again. The thoughts in my head were driving me crazy! I started writing this memoir. I needed to put my emotions somewhere. It seemed too complicated, to just try to talk to someone.

After contemplating who my mother really was, I had to ask myself if she may have been responsible for my low self-esteem, which had led to my excessive drinking problem. I had always believed that she was my anchor, but maybe that was deceiving. My dad and sister could stir up the household from time to time, but maybe there was a less obvious and quieter force at work!

Barb (Mom)

Phil (Dad)

PHOTOS I

Mom & Dad/Engagement

Mom & Dad/Sweethearts

PHOTOS I

Phil/High School Basketball

Phil/Disability Discharge from Service

PHOTOS I

My 1st Birthday with Mom and Siblings

My Brother and Sister

Me at 6 Years Old

My Catholic 1st Communion

Me & Sassy at Camp Property

Me & Sassy at Camp Property

An Older Dad at Camp Feeding the Deer

The Camp

PHOTOS I

Mike & I's Engagement

Me in My Wedding Dress

10

BELIEFS

My first year of sobriety was a year to explore my personal beliefs. As I mentioned, I grew up Catholic. I went to church every Sunday growing up. My dad never missed, and he would never let us kids miss either. I received my first communion and my first confession. I attended catechism, schooling where you learn about God, Jesus, Bible Stories, and the Ten Commandments. This is Christian teaching.

I know there are many people who embrace religion, and it enlightens their lives. If it makes them feel good about themselves, then all the power to them. I was just not one of them. I started researching other faiths and beliefs. I still wasn't happy with any one belief, so I came up with my own. You might say, a little of this and a little of that! But I do still adore Jesus at Christmas time. The world is a better place because he was here.

My interpretation of the message from Jesus's disciples is that they depicted Jesus as being the only way to obtain enlightenment. My interpretation of the message from his disciple

Thomas, is that he depicted Jesus's words to mean that we can obtain enlightenment by doing deep soul searching of oneself. The definition of *soul searching* according the Merriam-Webster Dictionary is "The activity of thinking seriously about your feelings and beliefs in order to make a decision or to understand the reasons for your own behavior." The book *Beyond Belief, The Secret Gospel of Thomas*, written by Elaine Pagels, is a good book to read about the disciple Thomas.

It was important to me to come to my own conclusions about faith. I questioned why we are all here. I think of God as an energy force, not as a figure sitting on a throne. An energy force that we are all a part of and connected to. I believe there are energy forces that we cannot see. I believe in angels, but I don't necessarily believe they have wings. However, I do like my figurine angels and fairies that have wings. I have a collection. But to me they are just symbolic of these energy forces.

I don't believe in Hell. I believe bad people are reincarnated almost as soon as they die. I believe bad people return to live life's lessons again and again. I think it is possible that there are dark souls amongst us who never learn. I believe we all return for life's lessons, but bad people don't get the vacation in Heaven like most of us do. In our reincarnations, we can come back with any genetic or biological makeup. We have new personalities based on our new environments. Despite the changes, the core of our true being still comes through!

I do believe that we all eventually go to a better place, the place most of us refer to as "Heaven." I believe it is in another dimension around us. The vibrational frequencies are too fast for most human senses. But I believe there are some individuals who can tune into it. I believe there are legitimate psychics, but I also think there are probably more fraudulent psychics. We all have the capability to tune into our psychic abilities through meditation and calming our minds. But for most of us, it is difficult. It seems to come naturally for a select few for whatever reason. Some seem to be born with the gift, so maybe in some cases genetics play a factor.

During my first year of sobriety, I became interested in psychics. I found a psychic in Milwaukee and decided to make a visit. She did a tarot reading on me. I was impressed by some of what she said. In her reading, she said that I had been recently hospitalized. This was true. The psychiatric treatment program I had been in had taken place in a hospital.

This perked my interest in tarot cards. The psychic shop offered a tarot reading class. I signed up for it. It mostly involved learning about the meaning of the cards. Anyone can do that, but it takes someone more gifted to be able to psychically read and make predictions about what the cards are saying. I don't even remember the meaning of the cards anymore. It was a long time ago.

I also signed up for a psychic class. I liked the meditation exercise where we focused on a single color to see its polarity color (its opposite). Polarity colors would be the same as the complementary colors on an artist's color wheel.

When doing this, you concentrate and focus on one color. An example would be to focus on the color red. You would then be able to see the color green around the red. Another would be to focus on the color yellow. You then be able to see the color purple around the yellow.

The surrounding color is not actually there. But you are not just imagining the color in your mind either. If you were to close your eyes, you wouldn't see it. I don't completely understand it myself, but I know this is a real phenomenon.

You're probably thinking that this is weird! The psychic told me that a lot of people cannot do this. But I was able to, as well as the other person in my class. Give it a try, it might work for you. Add some incense and some soft music. Turn off all technology. Use anything that will help you focus and relax. It's better to try it when you're alone, so you have less distractions. Using a small strip of colored paper works well to focus on.

I visited a couple other psychics in more recent years. One was shortly after my dad died. It was a spur of the moment decision. There was a psychic at the county fair. I decided to stop in. This psychic asked me if someone close to me had passed away in the past six months. I was impressed with that question because my dad had just died about two months prior to this. In my lifetime, I hadn't known many people who had died.

The psychic said that Dad was showing her that he wanted to give me a medal. The first thing I thought of was the medals he had received in the service, like his Purple Heart. At first, I thought maybe he wanted me to have one of his medals, because the psychic said, "He wants to give you a medal." My brother Barry has all of Dad's medals. He is his only son. In retrospect, I don't think what she said was meant to be taken literally. I believe this was symbolic of my dad telling me that he was proud of me. This was a better gift than a piece of metal! I had been sober for approximately ten years at that time. I was also dealing with a child with autism. This reading meant a lot to me!

I believe it might be possible for our departed ones to visit us through animals or other living things. They might also flicker with electrical lights or equipment.

While I was staying at my mother's home during the time of my dad's funeral, there was a stray cat hanging around the house for a couple of days. It had been meowing under the windows. Being that my mother, sister, and I are all cat lovers, it would have been a good way for Dad to get our attention. When I was in the garage with my brother's wife, Lydia, the cat came in. Both she and I were able to hold this cat. We both believed it to be Dad. My mother came out into the garage with us and we gave the cat to her to hold. The cat flipped out and scurried away. Then I thought to myself, *It must not be Dad.*

But now, I still think it may have been, because I believe my dad may have been upset with Mom when he passed. That whole, "Your mother, she is not as she seems," comes to my mind.

I also visited a psychic just two days after my mother died. This is fifteen years after my last visit to one. I didn't receive an intimate message from my mother. However, it was still interesting. The psychic told me that my teenage daughter was going to have a baby by the end of the year. She said my daughter was going to have a daughter. She told me I was going to be a grandmother. I wanted to be a grandmother, but I wanted my daughter to finish college and get married first. I really didn't believe the pregnancy was going to happen. I was right.

But interestingly, that following weekend at my mother's funeral, a cousin of mine told me that his teenage daughter was having a baby girl at the end of the week. This cousin was close to my mother. My mother would have been excited for them. She would have wanted to share the news about this birth with me. Mom would have told me about it on one of our phone calls, if she had lived longer. Maybe the psychic did receive information from my mother and thought it was for my immediate family, instead of my relatives. I know that's a stretch. But who knows!

The psychic said that our departed ones usually only come through with personal messages if there is something left unsaid. Mom told me during her last days in the hospital that she was proud of me for how I was taking care of Kyle. She also brought up how many years I'd been sober, approximately twenty-five years when she passed. Mom seemed to know those were her last days. She was putting her business in order.

This psychic also said to me, "You have a secret." She was right about that. My son with autism wasn't a secret, but I always kept my past alcohol problems private.

I do believe our departed loved ones watch over us. I believe we have guardian spirits. I believe we are on this earth to enlighten our souls. We are here to learn. We gain wisdom and knowledge while we are here. This may mean suffering or a significant challenge in our life. There are so many ways a person can suffer in this world. We all experience it one way or another. Everyone has something! I don't believe we are being punished. Suffering brings growth, and growth brings enlightenment. The phrase, "You have to fall before you can fly," by Kellin Quinn is so accurate.

SUBTLE SABOTAGE

I think of Earth as a huge school or university. We are all here to climb the ladder of education to strengthen our souls and eventually achieve enlightenment. Darker souls can take much longer to climb the ladder. They might not ever get very far.

Some souls strive for greater challenges or higher degrees, as one would in any educational system.

For a short time, I had a Buddhist friend. This Buddhist friend had a daughter who was in the same dance class as my daughter. I met her while sitting and watching my daughter in her dance class. We started a friendship, and I eventually attended a few of her Buddhist get togethers at her home. I learned about nirvana. Nirvana is like Heaven. It is the highest state that one can attain, a state of enlightenment, meaning a person's individual desires and suffering go away. There would be no more need for reincarnation. In my beliefs, this would be graduation, making it to the top of the ladder. It would be an eternity in Heaven in the Christian faith.

I'm not thrilled with the term *karma*. It makes it seem like we are all being punished, like an eye for an eye. It states it is the law of cause and effect. We reap what we sow. There is too much karma in the faith of Buddhism for my liking. There are a lot of people suffering in this world, and I don't believe they are all working off bad karma. In Buddhism, you work off your bad karma until you reach nirvana. It is a process.

It is not the process I believe in, where you are simply working to further your education through reincarnation (strengthening your soul through experiencing life challenges or suffering) until graduation (enlightenment). If you don't learn, you don't graduate (you don't have an eternity in

Heaven or be in a state of nirvana). You would then be left to continuously reincarnate and learn. You would never experience tranquility and peace of the soul. The tranquility and peace that comes from the light energy force that we refer to as god.

After a succession of lifetimes of reincarnation in which there is virtually no growth or advancement into the light, I believe that dark souls eventually become obliviated. But this is probably very rare, because even most dark souls experience positive growth. I think that dark souls would have to be exhibiting malicious acts indefinitely without any remorse to be permanently wiped out of existence from reincarnating here on Earth and from the astral world. Unfortunately, these extremely dark souls probably do exist!

This probably all sounds way out there, but I think a place called Hell with flames and fire is a bit way out there too! People's beliefs are a personal matter, although I'm sure that atheists probably think that all our spiritual beliefs are quite crazy! They are good people, but they cannot quite get a handle on something that is not proven. I guess that is why they call it "Faith!"

These are my beliefs My beliefs help to sustain me and my sobriety. If a person is happy in what they believe, I think they should stick with it. I'm not trying to influence anyone. I don't like people trying to influence me. I just want to share my thoughts about what I believe about this universe.

11

MOVING ON AND COMPLEX BIRTHING

After being sober for about a year, I started looking for a job. I had never worked before. I was thirty years old. I found a job working as a receptionist at a title insurance company. I did a lot of menial jobs, such as making copies, faxing, and recording incoming checks in a log book.

My main job was answering the multi-line phone. I think there were about ten lines. The lights would all start flashing at one time. I put a lot of people on hold when it got busy. I needed to take messages on the other lines. The quickest way to get rid of a call was to announce it over the loud speaker, but people were not always available. I did enjoy talking with the customers on the phone, even if it was only for a moment.

I made a good friend with the secretary at this title company where I worked full-time for two years. At my review, my boss told me that my most negative attribute was my handwriting. That was no surprise to me. I had been told that before. I don't have good handwriting. I prefer typing. My most positive attribute was that I got along well with all my coworkers.

My boss said, "Everyone likes you." That was nice was to hear. It is not always easy. People like to test you sometimes. I was starting to overcome some of my insecurities by this time. I was gradually overcoming my shyness. Life experiences have a way of knocking it out of you!

During the time I was working at the title company, I was also attending AODA (Alcohol and Other Drug Addictions) courses at Saint Martin's College in Milwaukee. I received a Certificate of Completion for an Alcohol & Substance Abuse Counselor Training Program. But I had never done an internship. My life was about to turn in a completely different direction: the world of autism!

I became pregnant with my second child. I mentioned my pregnancy to my friend, the secretary. I was planning to leave my job, but I was laid off instead. I soon realized that laying me off was a favor, because then I could receive unemployment for a time. If I had quit, I wouldn't have received it.

After being let go, I was home with my cats. I had previously taken in a stray cat that had hanging around my friend's home. The cat had turned out to be pregnant. I'd already had one cat, a stray we took in when we first moved to Wisconsin. The pregnant cat I took in had given birth to five kittens. I'd given two to my mother. She'd liked cats. Then I'd given one to my brother and his wife. I'd kept two, along with my other two adult cats.

Unfortunately, our miniature collie, Skipper, had snuck out of our apartment one day when we were carrying in groceries and was hit by a car. That was a sad day. I do love my pets. They love you unconditionally.

I was doing well with my pregnancy until the last couple of

months. During this time, I developed a mild case of preeclampsia. Preeclampsia symptoms are high blood pressure, water retention, and protein in the urine. Because of this, I also developed a cold and my doctor decided to induce labor just two days prior to my due date.

I have recently read that the drugs, such as synthetic oxytocin, used to induce labor, as well as the drugs used in an epidural can affect the immune system in an unborn child. I believe this weakened immune system may have made my son more susceptible to the effects of his vaccinations or the toxins they contained. *My theory is, it may have lowered his natural glutathione levels which help to detox the body of toxins.*

I had an epidural during my childbirth with Kyle. An epidural produces a loss of sensation below the waist of the mother. It is easier on the mother. At the time, I was told there was very little risk with an epidural. But because I had it done, I couldn't feel my contractions and had a hard time pushing. The doctor used a vacuum extractor device on the baby to pull him out. It is a soft cup attached to the baby's head with a suction. There may be some risk, but a baby's head during a vaginal delivery can also be traumatic. I have wondered if Kyle's birth circumstances started him out with a weakened immune system and with lower glutathione levels. Insult of the immune system can lead to further insult of the immune system.

My gynecologist insisted I have a vaginal birth with my second child. I'd had a c-section with my first child, Erik. I also had induced labor with him because he wasn't coming out. But it wasn't started until later in labor, and it was for a short amount of time. The baby was in stress, and the doctor decided I needed to have a c-section. With Kyle, inducement of labor started at the very beginning of labor and lasted all day. During the c-section with Erik, it was discovered that the umbilical cord was wrapped around his neck. That is why he wasn't coming out and why he was in stress. But there hadn't been any loss of oxygen to the brain. I'm glad I had a c-section with Erik. I wish I'd had a c-section with Kyle. It would have meant more pain and healing time for me, but it may have been worth it. But it is possible it may not have made any difference, or maybe he would just not be as low functioning as he is.

With my daughter, Krystal, I had a natural childbirth. I was thirty-seven years old by this time. I was given nothing. But I was starting to have trouble. I knew something was wrong. I asked for drugs for the pain. I wasn't given any. I pushed very hard, for my life. Krystal came shooting out like a football! The doctor literally had to catch her. I'm grateful she didn't fall on the floor. My baby was safe, but now I was shaking something terrible. I told the nurses I was shaking. They checked my blood pressure. I was told that it was extremely high. One of them said to me, "You're tough!" They then put a bunch of heated blankets over me to stop the shaking. It did help.

During my pregnancy with Erik, Mike was furious with my mother because there was an occasion where she had been encouraging me to have a glass of wine. She said that it was okay for me to have just one glass. But I was an alcoholic! She was very much aware of that. I never drank during Erik's pregnancy. As I mentioned earlier, I quit completely for those nine months. Unfortunately, I started up again a few months after he was born. By the time I was pregnant with Kyle and Krystal, my sobriety was in a solid place. Currently, I have over twenty-eight years of sobriety.

12
CHEMICAL DESTRUCTION

Kyle received all the required vaccinations during his childhood, as did my other two children. Boys, in general, are more susceptible to developing autism because of the mix of testosterone and thimerosal, a preservative in vaccines. Testosterone enhances thimerosal or mercury. This mixture lessens glutathione. Estrogen does the opposite. Estrogen can increase glutathione. It can help to protect the body from the negative effects of the poison. But that does not mean that girls are exempt from developing autism. Boys are just more susceptible and have a higher chance of developing it. Some people, in general, have more glutathione than others. This would explain why not everyone develops autism from being given vaccinations. Glutathione helps rid our bodies of free radicals, such as heavy metals. I learned this information from watching the documentary *Trace Amounts*, narrated by Eric Gladen.

Currently, flu shots still contain thimerosal. Even though thimerosal has been mostly taken out of childhood vaccinations in the U.S., they can still contain trace amounts. These trace amounts mixed with other toxins, such as aluminum, can enhance these poisons' negative effects.

Also, the younger the child who is getting the vaccinations, the more they might be susceptible to negative effects. The more developed system of a child, the better. But sometimes that is not even enough.

The number of children with autism has increased dramatically. In the 1970's and 1980's, about one out of every 2,000 children had autism, according to WebMD. In 2018, the CDC determined that approximately 1 in 59 children are diagnosed with an autism spectrum disorder.

In the book *Vaccines on Trial, Truth and Consequences*, written by Peirre St. Clair, he states, "Before 1970, American kids were fully vaccinated with 2 shots. By 1986, it was 10 shots. Today kids have to get 24 shots before the age of two." Plus, he states, "Today the federal government says that all children by the age of 18 should have 69 doses of 16 different vaccines. And 49 of those doses are given before age 6."

Thimerosal was taken out of vaccines in the United states in 2001. Kyle was born in 1995, and thimerosal had still not been taken out of childhood vaccines. There was a huge rise in autism in the 1990's. I truly believe Kyle would have been normal if it hadn't been for the vaccines, or more specifically, thimerosal combined with aluminum and the many other sabotaging ingredients. Erik was born in 1987, before the big rise in vaccines. Krystal wasn't born until 1999, after most of the thimerosal was taken out of childhood vaccines.

It would cost more to use safer ingredients in vaccines, but it would probably cost less than all the damage control costs for the victims. The medical community says they have taken thimerosal out of the immunizations. But they still use that minuscule amount, and it does not take much of a highly toxic chemical to have an adverse effect on a tiny baby. They also use aluminum, which is combined with other deadly poisons that make it more lethal. A couple of the other sabotaging ingredients in vaccines are antifreeze and acetone (fingernail polish remover). There are many more.

The combination of the thimerosal in vaccines, MMR vaccines, and other poisons have created havoc on our children!

As stated, there is still the mercury-containing compound (thimerosal) in flu shots, which are recommended to the young and old, and to pregnant woman. Flu shots are not even very effective. You can get the flu whether you have the shot or not. Typically, it is the people who already have a compromised immune system that die of the flu.

In my opinion, these agencies increased the amount of recommended flu shots for the very young to make sure children were still getting thimerosal in some form, otherwise the autism rate would decrease, and people would figure it out. Again, that is just my viewpoint of the situation.

I found an article written in June 2018 by bestselling author Sarah Pope, "The Healthy Home Economist." You can find it online under "Six Reasons to say NO to Vaccinations." The type of ingredients they put in vaccines is unbelievable!

There are many informative books out there now regarding the dangers of vaccines. A few of them are "Thimerosal, Let the Science Speak," by Robert F. Kennedy, "Master Manipulator," by James Ottar Grundvig, "Jabbed," by Brett Wilcox, and

"Vaccine-nation, Poisoning the Population, One Shot at a Time," by Andreas Moritz.

In the old days, it was normal for people to have measles, mumps, and chickenpox. People were not afraid of it. Deaths were rare. Then after having one of these diseases, you were forever immune. Back in the days of polio, parents were giving their children teething powder that contained mercury for their pains. Back in 1892, there was also a new pesticide, lead arsenate, that contained lead and arsenic. In addition, people were spraying their children with DDT (a deadly pesticide) to keep away insects. Is it possible that any of these poisons could have been the culprit for polio, or all of them combined? I obtained this information from the book *Unvaccinated*, written by Forrest Maready. I like this one because it is short and to the point. I highly recommend everyone to read these books. People need to be woken up!

It should always be the people's choice on what risks they decide to take with their own bodies and their children's bodies. People need to do what they feel is right for themselves and for their loved ones.

As stated, there are still minuscule quantities of thimerosal in childhood vaccinations, and it does not take much to damage a young child. The medical community gives too many and too much during a child's most vulnerable years. If you must have vaccines, I think they should at least be given after the child is a few years old, and they should be spread out. Better yet, they should make the vaccines safe, despite any increase in cost. These agencies are greedy!

Personally, I would rather have my child have the measles for a few days and be immune forever, than have them have an entire life of anguish and agony from autism. But I cannot go back in time. I had trusted people.

In my opinion, vaccines don't strengthen immune systems, they destroy them! They destroy the body's natural defense system. We might be less susceptible to other illnesses, such as the flu, if our systems hadn't been compromised. We are all being slowly poisoned by other means as well, such as pesticides, fluoride, and more. Kyle cannot tolerate fluoride either. I use a natural toothpaste to brush his teeth. He has not had a cavity in many years.

13

RUNAWAY AUTISM CHILD

When our son Kyle was born, he seemed like a normal baby. But when he was about six months old, I started to notice that he liked to hang his tongue out of his mouth. But I still didn't think much of it.

On a check-up with his pediatrician when Kyle was two years old, the doctor told me he should be talking more. He was hardly talking. She recommended we have him checked out by Early Intervention Services. We took him there, and they diagnosed him with sensory integration dysfunction. Today, this dysfunction is referred to as a *sensory processing disorder*.

According to WebMD, sensory processing disorder is when "the brain has trouble receiving and responding to information that come in through the senses. Some people with sensory processing disorder, are oversensitive to things in their environment."

They can become overwhelmed by sounds, touch or, sight.

Kyle couldn't handle being in places where there was a lot of noise. When a lot of commotion was going on, it was just too much for him. I remember taking him to a small circus that was in town. I was going to let him go into the bounce house for children. But he was already spinning out of control. My taking off his shoes made him go crazy. I had to carry him out screaming and crying over my shoulder. This wasn't the only time I would have to do this.

When Kyle was four years old, we decided to take him to a Developmental Pediatrician, who officially diagnosed Kyle with autism. She prescribed him the antidepressant Zoloft to try to calm him down. But he was only on it for two days when he decided to climb over our wired fence in the backyard. He had never done that before. At that time, I had him wearing an I.D. bracelet. I didn't know he was gone. This was in autumn. During the summer months I was accustomed to letting him spend some time in the backyard because the fence was padlocked. I would just look out the window periodically to check on him. But on that day we started the Zoloft, a police car pulled up to our house with Kyle in it. Thank goodness for the I.D. bracelet. Someone must have seen him and called the police. Later, I found one of his shoes still stuck in the fence. It didn't take Kyle any time at all to climb over the fence when he was on that medication.

Incidents like this made me feel guilty. I thought the medication was going to make him better, but it only made him worse. It was discontinued after that.

We had already decided sometime before this incident that it would be a good idea to put bolts on our front and back doors. We still use our bolted doors to this day. We need our keys to get in and out of our house. Our other children are accustomed to using keys as well. We also have a locked pantry closet and locked doors in the basement to protect our water heater, breaker box, and our other storage in the basement. Our refrigerator has a combination lock on it. Mike is an engineer, and he figured out a way to put one on it. This was needed because of Kyle's special diets. We couldn't have him getting into food that he wasn't supposed to have.

When you're raising a child with autism, you don't know everything you should or shouldn't do. It is a learning process. You tend to want to treat them like you would a normal child. Raising a normal child is a learning process as well, but a child with autism is much more complicated. Also, autistic children are all different from one another. What works for one, does not necessarily work for another.

Kyle attended Early Childhood Learning in the public school system. We also did ABA (Applied Behavior Analysis) for a year or so, where several women would come to our home separately to work with him. It kept Kyle occupied, and it provided some respite for me, but I cannot say that there were any changes. However, I appreciated these women's caring hearts!

We went to some local autism support meetings. I learned more about the biomedical side of autism. I learned about gluten-free and dairy-free diets from reading books. I tried the dairy-free diet first. It did seem to help somewhat. He was a little calmer, but still active. Before starting the dairy-free diet, Kyle had completely stopped using the few words that he had previously said. After taking away the milk, he started saying one or two words at a time again. Regarding his speech, that is still where we are today. He can say a few words at a time. I have continued the dairy-free diet all these years. I then tried the gluten-free diet. I didn't notice any difference in his behavior while doing this, so I discontinued it.

There are many good books and information out there explaining the biomedical side and treatments of autism. I have tried many of their suggestions. A favorite book of mine is *Children with Starving Brains: A Medical Treatment Guide for Autism Spectrum Disorder*, written by Jaquelyn McCandless, MD.

Jenny McCarthy also has a couple of good books on autism because of her own son with autism. They are, *Louder Than Words: A Mother's Journey in Healing Autism*, *Healing and Preventing Autism: A Complete Guide*, and *Mother Warriors: A Nation of Parents Healing Autism Against All Odds*. I admire Jenny McCarthy for her courage and fortitude in leading the path for parents to speak their minds regarding their autistic children.

It was a challenge trying to find things Kyle might be interested in doing while growing up, and it is still a challenge today. He wasn't interested in toys. He would just line them up. He didn't seem to have an appreciation for anything. I took Kyle to therapy sessions where he was able to spend time swishing around in a pool. He seemed to like that. It was a sensory-type therapy. He also started riding horses at a therapeutic equestrian riding center. He continued riding horses for sixteen years until we started having severe problems with his behavior. We discontinued the riding for a time. Thankfully, Kyle has improved, and he is able to ride again!

Kyle attended the public school system where he was in special education the entire day. In elementary school, someone from special education did assist him in a regular classroom. He had to have a one on one because he was a flight risk.

A music therapist started working with Kyle during the years he was in Early Childhood Learning. It was provided through the school. This continued for years, until Kyle left the high school at age twenty-one. It is something he enjoys. I would pay for it and take him to music therapy during the summer months as well. This gave me the opportunity to observe him during a session. It was heartwarming! This was the only time that I got to witness him using his voice along with a song. He does not carry a tune, but he does say most of the words to a song. Sometimes he almost whispers when he says the words, but that is okay. This is still big! Normally, you would only hear him say one or two words together, like "change please" (a diaper change). He can also say yes or no to questions presented to him. Kyle also had speech therapy through the school system, but it wasn't as effective as the music therapy. We also tried Picture Exchange Communication, sign language and other technical devices to aid with communication. In the end, the few words he would occasionally use seemed to work best. I have also relied a lot on my intuition and on how well I know Kyle's gestures and the noises he makes.

Kyle once sang "Frosty the Snowman" for the high school special education disability Christmas program. His teacher and aids were surprised to hear so many words come out of his mouth. A microphone was used so the audience could hear him. Again, he was just saying the words, not singing.

But again, that is okay! I was proud! His teacher and the aides seemed proud of him too! I also get very proud of Kyle when he rides horses!

In the school system, there were numerous special education teachers who tried toilet training him, but they were never successful. I had tried, of course, when he was younger. I even had the help of those women who came into our home, but it just wasn't happening. But wiping Kyle's butt has been the least stressful part of dealing with his autism. I have been desensitized.

Summers were hard when Kyle was little. For one month during the summer, he would attend a special education class. But this was only for a few hours in the morning. Although, it did still help.

I found a couple of day camps for children with disabilities that he could go to. One wasn't too far away. I'd drive thirty miles there, drop him off, and drive thirty miles back home. Then later that day, I would make the drive again to pick him up. It is about two hours of driving per day for one or two weeks of the summer. Kyle still goes to this camp every summer for at least one week. It is a good change and outlet from his normal routine. He enjoys going there!

The other camp he went to for a few summers was even further away. It was approximately 60 miles one way. It was a total of four hours of driving per day. Riding in the car has always seemed to calm him. We did that for one week out of the summer. I was desperate to find things for him to do! Plus, I needed the respite. Kyle no longer attends this camp.

For music therapy, during the summers, I would drive 45 minutes for a half hour session. Then another 45 minutes to drive home. Currently, the music therapist comes to our hometown to meet her adult clients. It is nice that I don't have to make that drive anymore!

During Kyle's adolescent years, we tried numerous medications. We tried stimulants, antidepressants, and antipsychotics. We tried Zoloft, Seroquel, Adderall, and Ritalin. They all made Kyle's behaviors much worse. We tried Risperdal for a couple of years, but that started to cause problems. I'll talk more about that one a little later. Regarding autism, Risperdal is a popular one.

I have also tried quite a few supplements with Kyle. Probably too many to remember. But here are a few of them. We tried Kirkman Labs Super Nu-Thera, a multi-vitamin specially formulated for autism. We had difficulties with that. I also tried numerous vitamins by themselves, such as vitamin B6, B12, C, prescription B12 shots, B1, C, folic acid, magnesium, etc. I also tried numerous herbal supplements on Kyle. All medications and most supplements have a negative impact on his behavior in one form or another. Some make him aggressive and controlling, some make him masturbate, some increase his sensory issues and he becomes aggressive in his touching of people or animals (squeezing to hard), some make him hyper, and some make him more obsessive compulsive. Some just make him act weird, where he makes these loud, irritating squawking noises. The good news is that the negative effects eventually pass!

The one herbal supplement I have found to be beneficial in small amounts is passion flower. I'm so grateful to have had a least one supplement that seems to be helpful. But again, less is better.

All medications and supplements I've tried were either

crushed, or a capsule was opened and put into a small amount of water. I administer by using a dropper. Kyle is amazingly cooperative with this procedure. He does not even flinch from the taste.

When Kyle was approximately eight years old, we took him to see a doctor, who was referred to by a DAN Doctor (Defeat Autism Now). But they don't really use that term anymore. These doctors are basically biomedical doctors who specialize in autism. This doctor has really been the only doctor who has understood Kyle and been able to figure out what might be ailing him. He has a son with autism himself.

I asked this doctor what he believed caused autism. He said it could be from genetics, environmental factors combined with genetics, or environmental factors such as the vaccines alone. Given the sudden traumatic increase in autism, I would think the environmental factors are at the top of the list!

Kyle had blood tests taken. It was discovered that he had elevated yeast/fungal metabolites in the intestinal tract. Specifically, he tested high with carboxycitric. He also tested somewhat high with arabinose. Kyle had candida albicans. Kyle has also had other skin and fingernail funguses to combat throughout his life.

To treat candida, additional diet restrictions were needed. Specifically, no refined or natural sugars. He was also given the antifungal compounded prescription nystatin for about twelve years, until the medication was discontinued. We never had a problem with it. They only offer nystatin without the compounding now. I don't know why, but this nystatin made Kyle aggressive. It was discontinued. Kyle gets probiotics for his candida. I have tried different brands, but the only one he has been able to tolerate is Pro-Bio Gold from Kirkman Labs.

Kyle was also tested for food allergies. He was only allergic to dairy/milk. His antibodies were high in this area. We had already taken away milk products years before.

Casein is a protein in milk, and gluten are proteins in wheat. As mentioned, we had already tried the gluten-free diet, and I didn't feel there was any difference in his behavior. The allergy test seemed to confirm what I felt about Kyle's non-reaction to gluten; he wasn't allergic to gluten or wheat.

The casein and gluten-free diet is recommended for children with autism because of a theory that they have opioid properties. Autistic children are often spacey. It is said that autistic children cannot digest the peptides (the unbroken peptide proteins affect the opiate receptors in the brain) from casein and gluten properly. It is an inflammatory issue.

Kyle had the Dr. McCandless Autism Panel done through our favorite (DAN) autism doctor. Dr. McCandless wrote one of the books about autism that I mentioned. Kyle's tests from the panel were normal, except for his antibodies being high in casein peptides. This is not another allergy test. This test is to check for elevated peptides. His test for gliadins peptides (gluten) was in the normal range. Again, I didn't see any reason to put him on a gluten-free diet.

We took Kyle to see another DAN doctor in Illinois. She did a hair analysis to check for toxins and heavy metals. <u>Kyle was high in arsenic, lead, cadmium, titanium, and nickel. He was also borderline high in mercury.</u> His overall score was very high in toxins. With these hair analysis tests, the scores may not even be as high as they really are, because the toxins are still in the body. Only so much comes out of the body's system into the hair, unless you use a chelator (detoxifying method) to rid the body of toxins. Then toxins might come pouring out.

This doctor wanted us to try to detox Kyle. We were given a transdermal glutathione prescription. Again, glutathione helps your body get rid of free radicals and heavy metals. We tried it for only a few days. The first couple of days it seemed great. Kyle was saying more words. But it didn't take long for Kyle to start becoming very aggressive. Also, a blood test indicated that his liver enzymes were high. It was discontinued. It was too hard on Kyle's system to have him detoxed.

Later, we bought an infrared sauna in hopes of detoxing him because it would be easier on his system. But Kyle would only sit in it for a couple of minutes. He does not stay in it long enough for it to do any good. He would need to do it continuously for the rest of his life in order for it to do any good.

When Kyle was eleven years old, he managed to escape from our house again. This time he took my keychain out of my purse and tried all the keys on the door lock. Kyle is smart! He found the correct one and was gone. It took about twenty minutes before I realized he was missing. I cannot remember if I was in the bathroom or what I was doing, but it was long enough for him to escape. I called the police. In just that short time, he had gone a few blocks from our house. There was a light rain that day. Kyle wasn't wearing his shoes. A woman saw him standing in her yard, flapping his hands and making noises. She was kind enough to invite him in. She gave him a few cookies and called the police. I had also called the police, so it wasn't hard to figure out where he belonged. Kyle was no longer wearing an I.D. bracelet because he would pry it off with a kitchen fork. This woman got her picture in the paper along with her story. Our names remained anonymous.

A few weeks after this, Kyle escaped again. This time, he broke out of our kitchen window screen. We called the police again. It didn't go as well this time. He walked into someone's home and startled them. I think he may have been looking for cookies! He wasn't permitted to have cookies at home because of his candida. After this incident, we put locks on our windows too. It would be years before we were brave enough to try letting fresh air in the house again. I also never keep my keychain in my purse anymore; I always keep it in my pants pocket now. Sometimes I feel like a warden!

Whenever we went to visit my mother, Mike and I were always worried that Kyle would escape. My mother didn't have bolts on her doors. I had suggested it once, but she completely ignored me. I don't think she liked the idea of ugly looking bolts on her doors for just the few visits we were there per year. But Mike and I could never relax when we were there, so we never stayed more than a couple of nights.

Kyle did escape from my mom's house a couple of times. The first time was during Thanksgiving. All the family was there, but no one saw Kyle leave. Several of our family members went out looking for Kyle. My nephew's girlfriend spotted him going into someone's house. She went over to retrieve him. No police were called.

Another time, I went to the bathroom for about two minutes and Kyle escaped. Mike and one of my nephews were also there, but they didn't see him leave either. My mom and my son Erik were just getting back from a store. They pulled into the driveway and Erik saw Kyle over at the neighbor's house. Erik got out of the car and ran over to get him. Erik said the woman was on the phone and it sounded like she was calling the police. Kyle's ill-starred fate continues!

14

SHATTERED IMMUNE SYSTEM

When he was in fifth grade, Kyle was put on a low dose of Risperdal. It seemed to go fine, except for the significant weight gain that it caused. In middle school, the Risperdal wasn't so fine anymore. I didn't see any extreme behavior at home, but apparently, problems were arising at school.

I wasn't crazy about one of his middle school teachers. The school district had always been very good to Kyle and my other two children. I would recommend any student to attend this school district. I had always felt that his elementary special education teachers had done well with Kyle. Not to mention his high school teachers. I didn't feel that way about this middle school special education teacher. I didn't feel that she communicated with me very well. I had always used notebooks to communicate back and forth with Kyle's teachers; it had always seemed to work well. (This was before texting, etc., became so popular.)

I first felt that something wasn't right while getting Kyle ready to go to school one morning. He said to me, "I'm scared," in a soft voice. This was very strange, because Kyle does not express how he feels. For the most part, he does not use words unless it's meaningless babble. I didn't know what to make of this.

I soon learned what Kyle was afraid of. I was called to come and pick him up from school. I went to his special ed. classroom, and his teacher opened a closet door. Kyle was on the floor, sitting in a small closet. They had a sensory room, but that was being used by other students. I wasn't given any details as to why Kyle was in the closet, but I was to find out that this was happening on a regular basis. I was infuriated! I wrote a letter to the school district complaining about the treatment. Specialists in dealing with autism came in to observe him and try to figure out a solution. The school district did try to rectify the situation, but I didn't understand why this was happening. Everything had been fine in elementary school. Kyle was starting to go haywire, and this teacher didn't seem able to handle the situation. She did leave her teaching position after that school year.

But I now knew that something was very wrong. I started to suspect the Risperdal. I was already aware that many of the supplements I had tried with Kyle might work for only a short time, then they would gradually start to affect him negatively. Most medications would affect him negatively immediately. Kyle had been on the Risperdal for over a year. I decided to try taking it away for a time to see what would happen, but I had a hard time doing that because there was still medication in the nurse's office at the school. In Kyle's communication notebook, I asked for his prescription to be sent home. An empty prescription container was sent home. After an angry message in the notebook to the teacher, the

Risperdal was finally sent home. Apparently, I needed to be more specific!

I refrained from giving Risperdal to him for a time, but then I tried giving him a very small amount one day to see what would happen. He was written up in gym class that day for pinching another student. That was my answer. It was time for the Risperdal to go.

During these middle school years, there was another camp that I used to send Kyle to during the summer. This one was close by. It took only about fifteen minutes to drive out there. Kyle had been going there for several summers. One summer that he was there, he completely freaked out. He viciously attacked one of the counselors by biting and scratching her. Again, there was nothing unusual happening at home. I was told that he had eaten almost an entire bag of carrots that they had there. Given Kyle's sensitive digestive issues, I believe that had been the problem. It was just too much roughage all at once for his sensitive digestive system.

Kyle had another incident during his middle school years. But this time, it was a completely different kind of incident. I had tried giving him oral chamomile to help calm his behavior. He started masturbating excessively from this. He was also going through puberty at the time, but this behavior was a bit extreme. He once leaned up against his speech therapist and pinned her to the wall. He also pulled his privates out on one occasion in the special ed. room. He had never done anything like this before.

I had to meet with the principal and his teacher. He had a different teacher by this time. I had to make Kyle start wearing suspenders to school every day. It was an effort to keep his pants up, although I'm sure he could have undone the suspenders if he really wanted to. But it never happened again. Kyle discontinued this behavior when I took the chamomile away.

This was a new lesson for me. I learned about how certain calming herbs could affect him. Some years later, we had some similar issues while giving him essential oils. So much for me trying to do something to improve his behavior. But this was nothing new to me. It seemed that mostly everything I tried to do to improve his behavior failed.

Kyle is also sensitive to anything transdermal. Any supplement, oils, medication, or product put into his skin can have negative effects on his behavior. Essential oils can also make him start masturbating. The transdermal glutathione I mentioned earlier had made him aggressive.

Bug sprays containing deet also make Kyle aggressive. Sunscreen also has a negative effect. I avoid putting anything into his skin if I can help it.

Kyle finally started to lose the extra weight he had accumulated during his time on the Risperdal. I had trouble finding jeans or pants for him to wear during this time. Because of the weight gain, Kyle started wearing sweatpants. But now that he was losing the weight, I wanted to put jeans back on him again, but he wouldn't let me put jeans back on him anymore. People with autism become stuck in their routines and ways of doing things.

I was happy when Kyle moved on to the high school. He had a really good special ed. teacher his first year. However, he was going to retire from teaching after that year.

During that year, Kyle had developed grayish looking blotches on his skin. They were on his arms, legs, chest, and stomach.

We needed to get a doctor's note for him to be able to go back to school. They needed to know if he was contagious or not. His pediatrician at the time identified the blotches to be acanthosis nigricans. This condition can be a sign of prediabetes. Diabetes is an autoimmune disease. Kyle's pediatrician wrote us a note to give to the school, and he was able to go back to school.

Around this time, I became soft in letting Kyle have just a few cookies every week. It wasn't a lot. But I had broken my own rules about not letting him have refined sugars because of his candida. I believe this is why he developed this acanthosis nigricans condition. The blotches went away and didn't come back after I discontinued the cookies.

But after finding out about the acanthosis nigricans condition, I was still concerned about Kyle getting diabetes. I decided to order a diabetic meter and test strips from Amazon. I started checking Kyle's glucose every morning. Kyle was cooperative about letting me prick his finger every morning. Most of time, his readings were fine, but there were a few times when it could go unusually high. There was also a time when it went very low. It was confusing to me. I had never known anything about diabetes before. I had to educate myself about it. My checking his glucose in the morning went on for a few years, but it is not even recommended that you check your glucose routinely when you have prediabetes. I no longer check him. If the acanthosis nigricans ever comes back, I would certainly start checking him again.

Around this time, another strange phenomenon was happening. Kyle's eyes would excessively water. His teacher said to me, "Kyle was crying today." I said, "No, he is not crying, his eyes frequently water that way." It was something I had been noticing for about a year. His eyes would water so much that if he blinked, tears came pouring down his face. But there was no red eye.

People suggested that it was allergies, but I don't believe that it was. It happened all year round. It happened during the cold, snowy winters. We have always had pets, but his eyes would be fine at home. But then Kyle would come home from school with his eyes dripping. But sometimes it did happen at home too. There didn't seem to be a clear pattern that I could pinpoint at the time.

He also has never had any other allergy symptoms, such as a runny nose or congestion. Only watery eyes! I remember once, when taking him to our favorite (DAN) doctor, his eyes were all drippy. The doctor was mystified by it also. We also had taken him to an ophthalmologist to check his eyes for any problems. Kyle didn't have an eye disease.

Kyle's pediatrician had suggested that he might have cholinergic syndrome. You have cholinergic reactions when a substance enhances the neurotransmitter acetylcholine in the brain. Some reactions or symptoms are diarrhea, urination, and lacrimation (watery eyes). It is a set of symptoms associated with poisoning from certain substances such as some medications, nerve gas, or insecticides. Kyle wasn't on any medications during this time. He certainly hadn't been in contact with any nerve gas. However, insecticides can be found in certain foods that have been sprayed with insecticides or pesticides, such as grains, etc. Most people can naturally detox these toxic substances from their bodies, but someone with a poor immune system might not be able to.

The opposite of cholinergic syndrome is anticholinergic syndrome. This is when a substance blocks the neurotransmitter acetylcholine in the brain. Almost every medication has anticholinergic activity in them, but some have more than others. Symptoms can include dry mouth, constipation, urinary retention, increased heart rate, and more. Anticholinergic syndrome can lead to delirium (disturbed state of mind and illogical thoughts), which includes confusion and restlessness. This last statement is important to me for what comes later for Kyle, our family, and his caregivers. In my opinion, Kyle will later go from cholinergic to anticholinergic. With Kyle's extreme sensitivities, there seems to be a fine line between these syndromes for him.

I came to believe that there was some connection between Kyle's watery eyes and his digestion. I would notice that his eyes would become increasingly watery after eating certain foods such as gluten or grains. Rice products seemed to also bring about the watery eye phenomenon. This would make sense if these grains were sprayed with insecticides! I have read on Google that they are indeed sprayed with insecticides. I believe the toxins in his food were giving him a cholinergic reaction. It may sound far-fetched, but there is a pattern with Kyle eating toxic food and his watery eyes.

During Kyle's second year in high school, he had another very good special education teacher. He had her for a couple of years. She was someone we already knew. She was one of the women who had come into our home to work with Kyle when he was little. She is also the one who was able to get Kyle back to wearing jeans again. I was grateful for that!

Kyle was now 18 years old. He was about to enter the independent living skills program, a special education class for 18 to 21-year-old disability students in the high school. Students in special education are permitted to continue in the high school until the age of 21. Kyle did receive a diploma, despite not being able to read, write, or do arithmetic in any way.

It was also time to go through the critical steps in obtaining legal guardianship of Kyle. It was a fairly easy process in our case, with Kyle being so low-functioning.

I take care of Kyle's personal hygiene and prepare his food. In addition to wiping his buttocks and changing his diaper, I need to shower and dress Kyle every morning. If I let Kyle try to pick out his own clothes, he might choose to put on shorts in the winter or a sweatshirt in the summer. He does not know enough to take off his jacket if it warms up in the afternoon.

He can put clothes on himself, except for socks. I buy Velcro shoes for him because he cannot tie shoes. But he might put a shirt on backwards. He also isn't be able to set the temperature of water for a shower; he might get scolded. He also isn't able to brush his own teeth properly. One small little swipe is not good enough.

A woman from the court came to meet Kyle and speak to us about guardianship for Kyle. Plus, someone was appointed Kyle's attorney and she came to meet Kyle and speak with us as well. When we went to court, there was no doubt in anyone's mind that Mike and I should obtain co-guardianship. Erik became the stand-by guardian if something should happen to the both of us. He wouldn't be his caretaker, but he would oversee his well-being.

The process felt a bit strange since we had taken care of him all his life. But legal guardianship is to protect the disabled individual, and any Social Security benefits he will receive. Everything must be reported to the court annually. There is a good amount of paperwork that needs to be done when you have a child with a disability.

Kyle began the independent living skills program at the high school. He had a great teacher during this time! I was very impressed by how much this caring teacher seemed to want to help his students. He even went to watch Kyle ride the horse one week at the equestrian therapeutic center. I'm sure Kyle enjoyed having him there. I really appreciated his interest in Kyle. After Kyle's first year with this teacher, we were asked to write something positive about him to help him receive an award. I was more than happy to write something positive about him. I'm sure many others did the same. He did receive the award.

During Kyle's first year in the independent living skills class, there was an issue with the school nurse. I was still checking Kyle's glucose levels every day during this time. The nurse was concerned about Kyle having diabetes. I had informed Kyle's teacher about my concerns of him possibly developing diabetes. I had informed him that I was checking his glucose every day. Kyle was sent down to the nurse's office a couple of times. I had to go to the school and pick him up a couple of times. His teacher or the aides must of thought that he didn't look well or wasn't acting like himself. But he wasn't sick.

After one of the trips down to the nurse's office at the high school, I made an appointment for Kyle to go to the doctor's office that same evening. It was regarding the possible diabetes issue. We were able to get in, but it wasn't with our primary pediatrician. This pediatrician wasn't concerned about Kyle having diabetes. He said that he had diabetes himself. He understood glucose readings.

At an annual IEP (Individualized Education Program)

meeting at the school, which included the school nurse, I was asked to buy and bring test strips to the school. I declined. It wasn't something that was being paid for by insurance. Kyle didn't have a medical diagnosis. I paid for his meter, lancets, and strips myself, that I used at home. But diabetes was still not really an issue that anyone had to be concerned about at that time. If Kyle's glucose readings at home had become alarmingly high or low on a regular basis, I would have immediately taken him to a doctor.

I was asked to bring in a note from a doctor stating that it wasn't necessary for the school to check his glucose. I made an appointment with an endocrinologist, a diabetic specialist. Mike took a day off from work. Again, a knowledgeable person wasn't concerned about Kyle having diabetes. I got my note from the doctor to give to the school. After this, I started to gradually stop checking Kyle's glucose. As stated, I no longer check him regularly. It seemed that all I needed to do was make sure that he didn't eat natural or refined sugar. The acanthosis nigricans skin condition has never come back.

When Kyle was young, I could handle taking him to his annual appointments to the pediatrician by myself. As he got older, with other problems arising, Mike would have to take off work to help me. Mike always has helped me with taking Kyle to the dentist. The dentist office has a specialized body wrap to keep him from moving. It is for his own protection. It really is not bad. It is sensory stimulating for him. It helps relax him.

When Kyle was little, he had to have some cavities filled. I made the mistake of letting him drink a lot of juice when he was a toddler. He couldn't have milk, so I substituted with juice that had calcium added. Thankfully, after I became strict about not letting Kyle have sugar anymore, there were no more cavities. But now he had a mouth full of mercury-filled cavities. I'm sure that didn't help with his issues. Neither did the sugar in the juice.

We were soon to venture on to another malady. I soon learned that Kyle had celiac disease, an autoimmune disease. When you have one autoimmune disease, you are also prone to developing others. An autoimmune disease is when your immune system starts damaging your own body. Environmental toxicity is a contributor to a faulty immune system. Arsenic, lead, nickel, cadmium, and mercury are included. Kyle's hair analysis for toxins indicated that he was high in all of these. The question is, where did they come from? Where did he receive such a high dose of these, that his body couldn't naturally detox them? Vaccines, of course!

15
CELIAC AND GASTROINTESTINAL DISEASE

At the core of Kyle's character, he really is a very sweet, caring person. Many of his caretakers, through the schools or day service programs, have been very fond of him. I have been told that he a great guy or "one of my favorites." When he is feeling okay in his own skin, it is not hard to be fond of him. He has a contagious smile. It is part of his charm. He likes to please others. I would have loved to have seen what he could have accomplished if he had developed normally. I believe that would have happened if he had never been vaccinated. I truly believe he would have been normal.

Kyle's second year in the independent living skills classroom wasn't any easier. This was the beginning of some aggression in Kyle's behavior. I think he was trying to control himself the best he could at school. But at home, I was starting to get attacked. Kyle would pinch me extremely hard. I had bruises all over my arms and chest. I would have to run to the bathroom and lock the door to protect myself.

Kyle was sending me a message. He always expected me to fix

whatever was wrong. Unfortunately, he is not able to use words to tell me when he has physical pain. When Kyle came home from school, I observed that his behavior would become very aggressive after he ate. He didn't eat much at school. During his first three years at the high school, he refused to eat any lunch. Looking back at this, I believe he did this to control his own behavior. This violent behavior at home would also happen on the weekends after eating.

During one of Kyle's attacks on me, I called the pediatrician's office in a frantic state of mind. I was crying and sobbing on the phone while I was talking to the nurse. I was recommended to call the crisis center, but the crisis center does not really do anything, unless you want to have your child brought to the jail.

I was looking for medical help! We went in to to see Kyle's primary pediatrician shortly after that phone conversation. I have always really liked this doctor. She is a good, well-meaning doctor, but she didn't have any answers for me on this one. Physicians tend to see autism behavioral issues as problems with their brains. That is what they are taught. They don't tend to think that, maybe, a person with autism might be in physical pain or discomfort and that they are acting out because of it. Physicians tend to think negative behaviors are only because of their autism and dysfunctional processing disorder, that they believe stems from the brain. A neurological disorder. Yes, as I stated earlier, a dysfunctional sensory processing disorder can affect an autistic person's behavior, but that is not always the case! People with autism have poor communication skills and cannot explain what their problems are, and they usually have multiple maladies!

I emphasized to the doctor that I thought he was acting out

because of the food that he was eating. Every day when Kyle came home from school, he would have a pepperoni and sausage pizza. I had given these to him for years. The mozzarella cheese on his pizza is the only dairy that I let slide because it is low is lactose. However, I have completely discontinued that now, too.

But no changes regarding his diet were made during that time. No solutions came from this appointment. I decided it was time to go back to our favorite DAN doctor. Kyle was now nineteen years old. We hadn't seen this doctor in years. Most of the testing we had done with him was when Kyle was eight years old. He was the only doctor I trusted to really listen to me.

He did listen to me. He ordered multiple tests to be taken from a blood draw. The only test that stood out was for celiac disease! It stood out a lot. The TTG-IgA normal range for this test was between 0.0-14.9. Kyle's test was >250.0. We were recommended to eliminate gluten. We also needed to schedule an appointment with a gastroenterologist.

We went to the gastroenterologist appointment, and then our next step was to have an endoscopic biopsy done on Kyle. He was sedated (I don't remember the name) with a liquid that we administered with one of our droppers. When this procedure was completed, the doctor came out and said that she didn't see anything abnormal in his intestines. I said to her, "But then why was his blood test for celiac disease so overwhelmingly high?" She didn't seem to know what to say to that. However, she did think that she saw something abnormal in his esophagus.

When the lab test results came back, it indicated that Kyle indeed had celiac disease. A microscope can see what the human eye cannot. It wasn't something I wanted, but I was very relieved to have an answer. It also made perfect sense as to why eating was causing violent behavior.

Kyle was also diagnosed with eosinophilic esophagitis. This is an allergic inflammatory condition of the esophagus. Symptoms include difficulty swallowing food, vomiting, and heartburn. We had noticed that occasionally Kyle would eat too fast and throw up some food, but this was very rare and seldom happened.

We were now recommended to see an allergist. This food allergy test wasn't as thorough as the first food allergy test we had done when Kyle was eight years old with our favorite doctor. But it did indicate again that Kyle was allergic to dairy/milk. Again, he wasn't allergic to gluten or wheat. The allergist wrote a prescription for Kyle to take the inhaler Inflovent. It is a steroid. It is prescribed for people with asthma. It reduces inflammation. However, it didn't work out. Kyle's obsessive-compulsive disorder went out of control. I wasn't happy about it, and Kyle's school teacher wasn't happy about it either. I discontinued the inhaler. I didn't feel that Kyle was having problems with swallowing food. He ate just fine. He wasn't deterred from eating at all. Vomiting was a very rare occurrence. It would only happen if he ate too fast and didn't chew his food properly. I would always cut up any meat that I prepared for him.

I was much more concerned about Kyle's irritable bowel syndrome, his celiac disease. All his life I had dealt with his constipation and diarrhea problems. These both can cause behavioral issues. Even today, if one of these is an issue, Kyle can go from being his sweet self to being a violent aggressor.

He charges at you, then he pinches and digs his fingernails into your skin. It creates bruises and marks.

For constipation, he gets Fletcher's Laxative for children. It is a liquid. He cannot take any other laxative because he will not drink enough water to make it work properly. He ends up in severe pain. You don't want to cause him pain! For diarrhea or upset stomach, he gets Pepto Bismol or Alka-Seltzer Gold. It must be Alka-Seltzer Gold because it is aspirin free. At night he gets melatonin to help him sleep.

If Kyle starts making intense high-pitched squealing noises and hand flapping, you need to run for the Alka-Seltzer Gold and Pepto Bismol. These noises usually indicate that he is in stomach pain. Natural or refined sugar can cause this to happen. Some intense hand flapping with deeper noises is usually constipation, which is not good either. Then you need some Fletcher's Laxative. Sometimes more minor constipation can cause him to be more sensory, where he tends to squeeze things, such as people or pets.

At times like these, I appreciate that he is still in diapers, because the only other way I can prevent these occurrences is by seeing what comes out of him or what does not come out of him.

In the past, I sometimes had to give Kyle an enema. I only did this if he was getting very agitated and hadn't had a BM for a few days. But one time, it didn't go well. I got kicked in the head. He didn't purposely aim for my head, but he did kick my head hard when he kicked out his legs. The whole side of my face was numb. But after a few days, it subsided. I did make a visit to a doctor after the incident. Another incident happened when I was changing him while he wasn't in a good way. He kicked out his legs and I went flying across the room. I was a little sore, but I was alright.

His pediatrician was sent Kyle's test results from the endoscopic biopsy, stating that he had celiac disease and eosinophilic esophagitis. I don't know why it never occurred to her that Kyle might have celiac disease. I had informed her of his constipation and diarrhea problems in the past.

I hadn't known what celiac disease was, myself, until after his blood test with the DAN Doctor. When I was called and informed by the nurse that he had celiac disease, I said to her, "What is that?" I have since educated myself.

Celiac Disease is an autoimmune disease that affects the small intestine. The small intestine is destroyed by the autoimmune system attacking itself. In the case of celiac disease, the villi in the small intestine is being destroyed. We need the villi to be able to absorb nutrients. As this worsens, damage can spread to other parts of the body. Gluten triggers the body to attack itself. To protect itself against the gluten intruder, the body inflames the villi. The body attacks itself. A good book to learn about celiac disease is *Celiac Disease, A Hidden Epidemic*, written by Peter H. R. Green, M.D. and Rory Jones.

People who have celiac disease tend to be deficient in vitamin D. This is an important vitamin for celiac individuals. It helps with inflammation of the intestines and a leaky gut. But Kyle cannot tolerate cod liver oil, which is high in vitamin D. His eyes become very watery and he becomes irritated. It is not organic. I believe that might be part of the problem. Kyle does get vitamin D from the organic eggs he eats every day.

With Kyle, it is more than just gluten that triggers intestinal problems. With Kyle, it is all grains. I believe it is the other grains that will become responsible for Kyle losing an unhealthy amount of weight. I believe this because his diet consisted of mostly gluten-free grains at the time. I will elaborate on his extreme weight loss in the next chapter.

Kyle was eating a lot of rice grains after his celiac diagnosis, not the gluten or wheat grains. The gluten and wheat grains were completely taken out of his diet. I will also go into more problematic issues of rice grains shortly. Problems such as being sprayed with pesticides.

I was starting to feel like no one (except our DAN doctor) seemed to want to acknowledge the connection between his autism and gastroenterology problems.

Dr. Wakefield, a gastroenterologist from the U.K., was let go because of his discovery of the connection between the MMR vaccine and gastroenterology problems.

I found an article from the *Age of Autism*, a daily web newspaper for the Autism Epidemic. The article is entitled, "Dr. Andrew Wakefield on The Poisoning of Young Minds," by Dr. Andrew Wakefield.

These few sentences of the article stood out to me:

"First, I will deconstruct the passage that the students are given to read."

"Autism is a brain disorder that can result in behavioral problems."

"Actually, rather than being a brain disorder, autism is a disorder that affects the brain. A growing body of published evidence indicates that for many children, autism is a systemic disorder affecting the immune

system, the intestine, and various metabolic processes such as those responsible for detoxification."

Dr. Wakefield's description of autism describes Kyle's afflictions to a tee! You can learn more about Dr. Andrew Wakefield from his books, *Callous Disregard* and *Waging War on the Autistic Child*.

Autism is a whole body phenomenon, but it seems like the medical community does not recognize this. Maybe because these issues have something to do with what they don't want to acknowledge. In my opinion, it is not really autism, but chemical poisoning. I believe that my child was overdosed with poisonous chemicals from vaccines. Kyle couldn't handle them. There are a growing number of children who cannot handle them. I don't think it's a coincidence that there is a growing number of children being diagnosed with autism. Many of the children diagnosed with autism also have a gastrointestinal disorder. It may or may not be celiac disease, but they have some sort of irritable bowel syndrome issue.

Dr. Wakefield suggested using single dose vaccines for the MMR vaccine, as stated in the documentary *Vaxxed*. But that wasn't acceptable with government agencies. The MMR vaccine program was more important than the safety of our children. Also, Dr. Wakefield suggested giving vaccines after children were a few years old, instead of when they were still vulnerable, developing infants. But that wasn't acceptable either.

There has been some recent research about children with gastrointestinal problems having fecal transplants. "Up to 50% of children on the spectrum are believed to have GI problems," according to a newspaper article written by Delthia Ricks. She also states, "Fecal transplants rebalance the microbial flora of the intestines—the gut microbiome—by providing recipients with the bacteria derived from the stool of a healthy person." I realize this all sounds rather unpleasant, but if it might work, it would be well worth it. In her article, she also tells of how the pharmaceutical companies are competing with physicians over how it should be administered. Big Pharma wants a piece of the pie, as usual!

16

EMACIATED

Kyle's diet changed dramatically after the celiac disease diagnosis. At first, I was buying all kinds of products that contained gluten-free grains. Rice was a popular one. I had also bought some corn seed grain products. I put some of those in Kyle's lunch bag for school. It didn't go well at school. Kyle became very violent and went after his teacher with the hard pinching and digging his nails into the skin. I was called to come pick him up.

His teacher didn't understand why these types of episodes had never happened with his previous high school teacher. I said to him, "Kyle didn't eat his lunch then." Kyle always had a lunch sent to school in his first years at the high school, but had refused to eat it. He would eat it when he came home. He was self-managing his own behavior by not eating. He didn't want to lose control of himself and hurt someone.

After this episode, Kyle continued to eat lunch. I took out all the corn seed grain products. In the past, I would never allow

Kyle to eat any corn, because it seemed to make him very upset. I had thought that it was too rough for him to handle. I hadn't given Kyle any corn or popcorn since he was a little boy. But I thought that if the corn was in a chip form that it would be okay, but it wasn't. I took the corn seed grain snack out of his lunch and it did seem to help with the aggression. But there were still problems. Kyle was gradually losing weight. I was still giving a lot of the rice grains.

That year, we brought Kyle to see a new DAN doctor who worked closer to where we lived. He put Kyle on Diflucan because of the candida issue. That didn't go well. Kyle didn't tolerate that at all. He had only been on it for two days and Kyle refused to get showered or change out his poopy diaper that day. I was afraid he would get a diaper rash. It was very unusual for him not to go through with his normal routine. Routine is very important to most autistic individuals. I wasn't able to send him to school because he wouldn't cooperate. Kyle was acting very lethargic and strange. He was pushing his face into his pillow, as if he was trying to smother himself and commit suicide. I had to wait until his dad came home to help me get him into the shower. That was end of that medication.

By the end of the school year, Kyle only weighed 112 pounds. His average weight had been about 140 pounds at 5'10" tall. Kyle had always been on the slim side, except for those couple of years that he was on the Risperdal. But now he was becoming emaciated looking. I knew that Kyle was eating plenty of food. He does pace around continuously and burns off calories, but this weight loss was something we had never experienced before.

Kyle's diet consisted of mostly gluten-free grains! We had him on the gluten-free diet, as we had been instructed to do. Mostly rice grains, protein, a little bit of cooked veggies to soften them, and a handful of almonds. I didn't understand his weight loss. I knew he had celiac disease. I could only think that somehow it was gradually killing him. I read that people used to die of celiac disease, but Kyle was now on the gluten-free diet, so how was this happening?

I cannot blame his teacher and the school for becoming very concerned about Kyle regarding his weight loss. It was understandable because this was a serious issue. I truly believe they were fond of him, and only wanted the best for him.

Someone from the school called Kyle's primary physician, his pediatrician, about his weight loss. I know this because the doctor's nurse told me. I told the nurse that they had my permission to talk to the school. But then the next thing I knew, someone (I don't have any official information as to who it was) reported Kyle's condition to the state. Kyle's doctor was being mandated to recommend a dietician for Kyle to see.

I'm the first one to admit, that logically, this sounds like a wonderful idea! But the problem is, someone who does not know Kyle is not familiar with his food sensitivities. I couldn't help but feel upset because I was scared for Kyle, myself, and the rest of my family.

I initially had declined the suggestion of a dietician when I was called by the state, but then it was mandated. I was very afraid of what kind of food would be recommended. I was very afraid it would only upset his sensitive bowel issues even more. Upsetting his digestion further wouldn't help him gain weight. This would have also caused him to start attacking me and our pets. (Thankfully, he never went after his sister.) He went after me, because in his mind, I was the only one who could make him feel better. However, sometimes it seemed as if he would try to stay away from me to avoid attacking me, until he just couldn't stand it anymore.

I envisioned the worst scenario. The thought of someone else telling me what I should or shouldn't feed him frightened me. I anticipated Kyle attacking me so often that we would have to institutionalize him. I didn't think that a group home would take him either. Then I imagined doctors giving him mediations to try to control his behavior. And then his behavior would only become much worse. I thought he would die in an institution, miserable and in severe pain. At home alone, I cried. The situation seemed hopeless. If his celiac disease was going to kill him, I at least wanted him to be at home with those who love him.

I know this thinking is a bit extreme, but Kyle's aggressive behavior can become a bit extreme. Kyle's teacher had experienced this aggressive behavior as well and was also alarmed by it.

My belief that celiac disease would eventually kill Kyle is what led me to the website that would be the answer for him. I looked up 'dying from celiac disease' on Google and found the article "The Gluten-Free Lie: Why Most Celiacs Are Slowly Dying" by Jordan Reasoner. This also led me to "The Toxic Truth About Gluten-Free Food and Celiac Disease," also written by Jordan Reasoner.

He lists a couple of reasons as to why other cereal grains can contribute to inflammation and a leaky gut. One being toxic prolamines. Prolamines help plants protect themselves from extinction by causing digestive problems in those that eat them. It cannot be broken down during digestion. Prolamines are in gluten and other grains as well. Plus, there are plant lectins, which are not digestible either.

With celiac disease, glutenous foods cannot be eaten, but there are other offensive grains that can also aggravate a celiac's digestion. In addition, sugar creates small intestinal bacterial overgrowth (SIBO) in your gut. This contributes to a leaky gut.

Jordon Reasoner's article has a link to the book *Breaking the Vicious Cycle* by Elaine Gottschall. She also wrote a great article, "The Gut/Brain/Food Connection: The Specific Carbohydrate Diet." You can look up the Specific Carbohydrate Diet online. It lists all the foods you can and cannot have. This is the diet that helped Kyle regain some weight. The Paleo Diet is also good, but I still need to be careful putting Kyle on these diets too. Every individual is unique! Kyle hadn't been able to eat the fruit or honey that the Specific Carbohydrate Diet says is okay to have.

In Elaine Gottschall's article, she states that grains contain starch. She states that her diet does not allow rice at all. The starch is another reason why Kyle may not have been able to handle all the gluten-free grains that are on the store shelves today, particularly the rice grains.

I started the Specific Carbohydrate Diet in May, and was able to get Kyle to gain seven pounds before our dietician appointment in July. He went from 112 pounds to 119 pounds. We were on the right track!

I left a message on the dietician's voicemail the day before our appointment. I wanted to inform her ahead of time about what I was doing. I wanted her to be able to have time to research it if she wasn't familiar with it. She appreciated my doing so, but she had already heard of the Specific Carbohydrate Diet because of just one other client she had. I thank God for that one other client! The dietician said if it weren't for that client, she would have been very skeptical of the diet. We were able to continue with this diet, and Kyle's weight went to about 144 pounds. He is still slim, but he is a healthy slim. His new primary physician was pleased! However, I do still have concerns about him losing weight again.

. In agreement with his dietician, Kyle is on a high-protein diet which consists of gluten-free ground turkey burger (no bun), lots of gluten-free chicken sausages, gluten-free, uncured turkey bacon, and eggs. But not one turkey bacon brand that we tried that contains honey, brown sugar, and pork. Kyle went absolutely wild and viciously attacked me after eating it for a couple of weeks. Apparently, the sugar building up in his system was too much!

This isolated incident was more recent. It had been several years since he had attacked me that way. It was a reminder of how it makes me feel. I had many bruises and scratches from him intensely squeezing my arms. He was so aggressive, I nearly called the police. Mike had already left for work. I was alone with him. The aggressiveness hadn't started until after he got out of bed.

It was difficult giving him his stomach pain relievers with the dropper I use to administer anything to him while he was attacking me. But I managed to get enough in him to calm him somewhat. I hid in the bathroom with the dogs until he calmed down. I was then able to give him more.

I was still able to function outwardly after this kind of

episode, but inwardly I felt paralyzed. I felt like I was walking around like a zombie! It is a traumatizing experience. Thank goodness it was a short-lived experience and his behavior is back to normal. This episode wasn't normal. I know this behavior was caused by intestinal pain. An episode like this is a reminder that his strict diet must stay intact, even if it has been many years since he has acted out like this.

Kyle also gets just a handful of almonds (too many is not good) and some cooked carrots. Raw veggies can be too high in roughage and cause gas.

Almond flour and coconut flour are too hard for him to digest as well. I have tried baking with them, but they are too hard on his system. Also, peanuts cause Kyle bowel irritation. His eyes water up. His food allergy tests indicate that he is not allergic to them. However, peanuts contain varying levels of aflatoxins, which are toxic compounds formed by a type of mold.

I tried watermelon and honeydew for a treat, but they contain too much fructose for his candida. I also tried using honey. After just a couple of days, Kyle was wailing in pain and in attack mode. Fruits also have this effect on him. The caveman diet seems to be the best approach for Kyle.

Kyle's digestion issues went haywire when I tried giving him gluten-free, uncured pork bacon. That is why I switched to turkey bacon. It had similar effects as the rice grains, in regard to the watery eyes. Having the watery eyes after eating pork was something I didn't expect. I researched online that the meat and fat of a pig absorbs toxins in a big way. More than beef or venison, because a pig does not sweat, and the toxins remain in its body. Our favorite DAN Doctor had mentioned that his son with autism couldn't tolerate pork. I wish I had heeded his advice. We have now switched to gluten-free, uncured turkey bacon. Kyle's food must be gluten-free, dairy-free, unprocessed, no preservatives, non-GMO, and organic.

Recently, Kyle got into artificial sweeteners, such as stevia and saccharin. He had the watery eyes from these as well. Apparently, these can be processed with toxic chemicals.

In addition to his watery eyes during these times, Kyle needs to excessively stim with hand flapping. He will obsessive-compulsively put in and out old animated VHS tapes out of the player as a coping mechanism. He will refuse to get his diaper changed or get showered and ready to go to his day services. It can take hours for him to come out of what he is going through. But he does come out of it after taking his Alka-Seltzer Gold. It is alkaline. I believe this helps him.

Despite Kyle being on a strict gluten-free and dairy-free diet for several years, he still has a very sensitive gut. The special diet does help, but it has not eradicated the gastrointestinal issue. Kyle has more than celiac disease. He has candida and most likely a leaky gut, a digestive condition in which bacteria and toxins are able to "leak" through the intestinal wall. I firmly believe that he has irritable bowel syndrome in addition to his celiac disease.

A few years back, we took Kyle back to our old favorite DAN doctor. I was still nervous about Kyle having pains during eating and digestion. The doctor prescribed Dicyclomine. This medication is an antispasmodic. It treats irritable bowel syndrome and inflammation of the intestines. Unfortunately, it is also a powerful anticholinergic!

Kyle had had the most fantastic year. He was now out of the

high school and was attending a day service program in our area. He enjoyed this so much! They did productive and fun activities every day. They did many field trips. The people at this day service program were absolutely wonderful! I thought we were set, and everything was alright in the world! I was wrong!

17

INSANITY

Gradually, Kyle's behaviors started to change. He started to control us. I remember him calmingly walking into my bedroom in the middle of the night and pulling me out of the bed. He pushed me onto the living room couch. Then he would pull me up again and push me into my chair. He kept repeating this. This was bizarre! I finally made it back to my bedroom and locked the door. He had never done anything like this before, and the aggression wasn't done in anger and pain like with the celiac disease. It was done with a straight face. It was almost zombie-like behavior!

Another morning, Kyle came into my bedroom and started to pull me out of bed again. I thought, *Okay, I'll get up*. But then he pushed me back into bed. I thought, *Okay, I'll stay in bed a little longer*. But then he was trying to pull me out of bed again. Back and forth we went with this, until Mike came to my rescue. Mike was already up and heard something going on. Mike had to restrain Kyle long enough for me to give him some calming supplements to help soothe him. Then I went into the bathroom to get ready for my day, but then Kyle was banging on the bathroom door. After this incident, I locked the bedroom door at night, regularly. Prior to this incident, I had never locked the bedroom door.

When this insanity began, I started to suspect the Dicyclomine medication. I knew that Kyle could be on a medication for a time and then it would start to affect him negatively. That is what had happened with the Risperdal.

To see if I was right, I tried taking the Dicyclomine away. It did help somewhat. Then his behaviors got worse again when I tried giving it back to him. This was my answer. I had to discontinue the Dicyclomine, but he had been on it a long time. It took a very long time for it to get out of his system. It was very disappointing because it had helped with gastrointestinal issues, and he had been able to eat better.

The madness continued for nearly a year. We tried other medications in an effort to help the situation. That was a mistake. They didn't help. They prolonged the situation.

If I sat in my recliner chair, he would get behind me and push on my back with his feet to make me get up. When I changed his diaper, we would go through a whole package because he couldn't make up his mind which diaper he wanted. He kept pulling them off. I had to start hiding diapers.

Kyle would pound on my bathroom door, sometimes with an object. There are marks all over the door from this. Sometimes he would sit on the floor and kick the door with his feet. He sprained his ankle doing this.

If I tried to escape outside, he would pound on the window of the back door. He managed to break it once. It was a good thing that it was a plexiglass window, not glass. I started leaving the house on the weekends for a few hours when Mike was home. He tried controlling Mike too, but he was the worst with me. At first, I would just drive around or go to a park, but then I started going to the theatre by myself. I hadn't been to the theatre for ten years. Now I was going every weekend. Sometimes my daughter, Krystal, came with me if she wasn't busy.

Kyle would make Krystal go to her bedroom when she was home. She also had a hard time using the bathroom in the morning. Mike had trouble with him pounding on the bathroom door too. Krystal was too nervous to even come out of her room and get something to eat.

Krystal wanted to attend her junior prom. I had bought her a beautiful dress. I was having a hard time helping her tie the corset in the back of the dress because Kyle was pounding on her bedroom door. It was a special time and I wanted that moment with her. He didn't want me in there. Mike intervened and I was able to get it done. Mike also had to intervene whenever I left the house or whenever Krystal tried to leave the house. Kyle wasn't letting us out of the house. Erik intervened and restrained Kyle a few times to help me out as well.

Kyle wouldn't let us watch movies that we rented. This was something we did on the weekends. We gave it up. Most of the time, he wouldn't let us watch TV either. Sometimes he would let us watch for a while, but then he would unplug the TV in the middle of a show. He would make me go to bed. I didn't resist because then I was free from him. I kept the door locked. I had a TV in the bedroom. I used headphones so he couldn't hear and wouldn't know I was watching T.V.

His day service program was also having problems. He was trying to control them too. He wasn't allowed to be with the group anymore. They were having problems, such as him grabbing the steering wheel when someone was driving, and not wanting to stop at stoplights. Plus, he would refuse to wear his jacket in the middle of the cold winter. It would be zero degrees outside, and he didn't care. All I could do was put a warm sweatshirt on him every day and get the car warmed up for him. Eventually, the owner of the day service program was able to put her husband's coat on him. Then soon after, he was willing to wear his own coat.

I'm just so grateful to the day service for sticking with him like they did! They have been a godsend! I wouldn't have made it through this time without them. I wouldn't make through caring for Kyle without them, period! Kyle would be lost without them too. The day service program activities provide the desperate stimulation that he needs. During this time, Mike and I were often talking about putting him into an institution. I didn't think that a group home would take him.

The owner of the day service program did ask that we take Kyle to a doctor. We got Kyle in right away. He had a new physician now that Kyle was an adult. He had only met Kyle once before. Kyle immediately starting pounding on a mirror that was in his office. The doctor immediately suggested that we take him to the emergency room at the hospital. The owner of his day service accompanied Mike and I that day. It took the three of us to try and control him. The emergency room doctors did tests that cost over $10,000 dollars that day.

Thankfully, he was on Mike's insurance until the age of twenty-six. Also, he had his Medicaid.

But they found nothing! One of the tests checked for a urinary tract infection. That was one test that the day service program owner had really wanted us to do. There had also been concern about this when Kyle was still in high school because of the dark color urine that he has. So, I really wanted that test done too. But the test came back negative. In my opinion, the darker color urine is from all the toxins in Kyle's system.

I didn't know what to do next, so I called our favorite DAN doctor about what was going on. He recommended the Risperdal again. I had thought about trying the Risperdal again when I needed to get Kyle to gain weight, but I had decided that it wasn't a good idea. We gave it a try this time, but it didn't work out well. At first, it did seem to calm him a little, but it wasn't long before his controlling, obsessive-compulsive behavior became even worse.

We were advised to see a psychiatrist. Interestingly, finding a psychiatrist who would take someone with autism wasn't easy. We did finally find someone. Kyle was prescribed a medication. We tried a couple of anticonvulsants. We tried Depakote first, for months, and then later, Lamictal. These treat bipolar symptoms and seizures. Again, Kyle's OCD (obsessive-compulsive disorder) behavior became even worse. We also tried Prozac, an antidepressant. It took several weeks before the Prozac kicked in, and when it did, he was into everything in the house. He would stay up all night going through drawers and everything else. He was also still trying to control us. The one common denominator is that all the medications are anticholinergic, especially the Dicyclomine that led the way. Kyle had been on it for nearly two years.

I had also been trying other calming supplements such as turmeric, lemon balm, and a quite a few others. But they became problematic too. Kyle would make weird squawking noises and become wound up.

After months of trying these medications and supplements, I decided to get rid of them all! I only relied on the one supplement, passion flower. Thank goodness I still had something to give him. He only needs one or two capsules per day. I open the capsules and put in in a very small amount of water. I then use a dropper to administer it to him. I might give him three or four on a bad day, but you don't want to give too much of this either because of side effects. Some herbs are natural antihistamines. Even these can have anticholinergic effects. When I give him too much, I start seeing those controlling behaviors come creeping in. The chamomile herb will do this even more than the passion flower. I will not give him chamomile for that reason. In addition to that, there is the masturbating issue.

There are some days where Kyle makes these continuous, irritating moaning noises. I'm not exactly sure why. He likes to say *do*, *da*, or *di* a lot. We find ourselves saying these back to him. He likes that. We joke about our family being cave people sometimes. A little humor helps!

Although we haven't had any luck with medications or most supplements, it is possible that they may work for others. I do know some people who say that medications help their autistic children. But I also know some people who say they have problems with giving their autistic children medications, as we do. I cannot say for a fact, but it appears as though the lower functioning the autistic individual is, the less likely they will be able to tolerate medications. In my opinion, the more damaged they are from the poisonous chemicals, the lower their tolerance for any further chemicals in their bodies. Their detox systems are too compromised. The bottom line is, autistic individuals are all different, despite some of their similarities.

A friend suggested that we try CBD oil. As of the time that I'm writing my memoir, you have to have a doctor's permission to use this in Wisconsin. First, I asked Kyle's primary physician, but it was a no. Again, I called our favorite DAN doctor. He said no at first, too. But I called back and explained to the nurse that it was legal in Wisconsin if you had a permission note from a doctor. I asked her to tell the doctor to look on Google. He did, and we got our doctor's note recommending the CBD oil for autism and anxiety. We tried the CBD oil with no THC for a couple of months, but it made Kyle wound up too. He was making those strange squawking noises again, like he did with some of the other supplements I had tried. I discontinued the CBD oil.

However, I have heard that it does help some people with autism. I do think that for those who the CBD helps, they should be able to just get it if they want to. That goes for everyone, not just people with autism. It does not cause a high, and it does not hurt anyone. It didn't hurt Kyle. But it did bring out some irritating behaviors.

Our new governor is proposing changing this law so that you can legally obtain CBD oil without a note from the doctor. However, it is confusing to me, because I already see CBD oil being sold in local stores. I hope that the change does go through for the people that feel it is beneficial for them. Not to mention, for the dogs and cats who might benefit from it as well! Our governor is also proposing medical marijuana. I hope that physicians will be willing to give it to those who need it, if the proposal goes through. But I cannot say that I approve of recreational marijuana.

When I asked our primary doctor about recommending the CBD oil, it was suggested that we try Clonazepam. It is in the class of drugs called benzodiazepines. It is highly addictive, but it is calming, like valium. I was very nervous about trying anything that was addictive. It was important that I was able to take away anything that didn't work and caused problems, which was usually the case! I tried half a tablet of a Clonazepam one evening and Kyle started biting himself. This is another behavior that he displays when not feeling comfortable in his body. I never tried the Clonazepam again.

Gradually, Kyle's behavior was starting to improve after taking away all the medications. Our old Kyle was starting to come back, but it was slow and gradual. It was if he was going through withdrawal. But even though his controlling behaviors and OCD were not as bad, he still had a lot of anxiety. This is when we tried the CBD oil. It was during this high anxiety period.

Kyle also did a lot of pacing and chewed on objects consistently. He chewed holes through his shirts. I bought him some sensory chew necklaces. It didn't take long for him to go through them, and I had to buy more.

Kyle also excessively fiddled with items until he broke them. He broke many of my knick-knacks I had around the house at the time. He has broken two of our TV sets. One of them he broke with one swift whack with the remote control on the screen. He would also pick up objects in the house and drop them somewhere else in the house. Our hallway was a favorite place for him to drop things. Sometimes it was my knickknacks, silverware, or just about anything in the house. It was like, "Where is my spatula? I'll go look in the hallway and see if it's there. Oh, there it is!" As frustrating as this behavior was, it was an improvement over what we had been going through with the controlling aggressive behaviors. Eventually, the OCD controlling behaviors and the withdrawal anxiety diminished. He still has OCD and anxiety behaviors, but not to the extreme that they were. At least, not on a daily basis. Life is still very challenging in caring for Kyle and can be very difficult at times. He is unpredictable!

We took Kyle in for his annual check-up with his primary physician. They were impressed and probably relieved by how well he cooperated and behaved.

We are still dealing with Kyle's usual autism behaviors, but we are accustomed to those behaviors.

At his day service program, he is gradually getting to do activities with the group again. He is participating in music therapy again. Hopefully, he will be able to ride a horse again regularly. He has had a few trial runs on riding the horse and he did very well. It was sad to discontinue that activity after sixteen years of riding.

I love my great state of Wisconsin for the wonderful disability programs that we have. The programs we have here support the parents or guardians, so that they can help to take care of their own. Otherwise, they might not be able to. They might not have a choice but to put their loved one in a group home or an institution. The parents need to be able to survive too. It is more costly for a state if the state must take full responsibility for these disabled individuals.

At Kyle's next annual doctor's office visit, I was asked what I had done to improve his behavior. I said, "I did nothing." It was *time* that was healing Kyle. It took time for all the effects of the medications he had been on to get out of his system. Particularly, the Dicyclomine that he had been on for almost two years, which had been prescribed to help him with the pains of his gastrointestinal inflammation. It may have helped with the inflammation, but it wreaked havoc on his brain.

Dicyclomine is an anticholinergic. It is high in anticholinergic properties. Every day, Kyle had taken a high dose of this drug. The other medications he'd been on also have anticholinergic properties. Plus, Tylenol PM is an anticholinergic. This was something else that I used to give Kyle at bedtime. I will not give this to him anymore either. All antihistamines have anticholinergic properties. Most medications contain some amount of anticholinergic properties.

It is my opinion that Kyle was experiencing anticholinergic syndrome. Anticholinergic drugs have been known to contribute to Alzheimer's Disease and dementia. The behaviors for anticholinergic syndrome again are delirium, a disturbed state of mind, illogical thoughts, confusion, and restlessness. These symptoms seem to perfectly describe the behaviors that Kyle was displaying. It was if he had gone temporally insane!

I became certain that this all happened because of the Dicyclomine and the other medications. Time off the medications was what he needed to heal. The Tylenol PM I had been giving him to aid his sleep contributed to the problem as well. I can still give Kyle melatonin at bedtime to help him sleep. Thank goodness!

I must emphasize that despite the improvement, Kyle is still severely autistic and his behavior can still be very unpredictable. It is crucial that he has "one-on-one support" at his day service program, camp, and wherever else he is. He is not only a possible flight risk, but his worst behavior would surface if he didn't have that individual support. It wouldn't only affect him and his behavior, but everyone around him.

18
MY DYNAMIC OFFSPRING

When Kyle was an infant, I looked at him and thought he was a higher soul. I may have been right with everything he has had to go through in his life. Underneath his agony of autism is a bright, goodhearted young man. He can be very sweet at times! I looked at Erik as being a prince or a king. That might be partly because he was our only child for eight years. Plus, he has a persona of leadership about him. Maybe a little of the Scandinavian God of Thor, when it comes to him protecting his family and friends. Krystal is my Supergirl or Wonder Woman with all her sparkle. She is also a leader. I'm so very proud of all three of my children. I love them with all my heart! This includes their father, my husband, Mike!

My three children were years apart in age. Erik was eight years older than Kyle, and twelve years older than Krystal.

It has been hard for my other two children to grow up with a brother who has autism. Erik was eleven years old when Kyle was born. He was living out of the house by the time Kyle's more undesirable behaviors began. But that is not to say that we didn't still have struggles to live with during the time Erik was still living in our house.

But Krystal has had it rougher. She has been in our home her entire life with Kyle, but it has not always been rough going. When Kyle and Krystal were little, Krystal would try to do things with Kyle. I remember them being in this small pool I had for them in the backyard. Krystal would try to entertain Kyle by having him imitate what she was doing. It was cute to watch.

I describe Krystal as exuberant. She likes her extra-curricular activities. I think a part of the reason Krystal has involved herself in so many ventures might be because she wants to be out of the house. I think this was especially true during her last few years of high school. This is when Kyle started becoming worse with his controlling behaviors. But it is also true that Krystal has always just been one to want to be involved in activities. But I'm sure being so involved in other activities has helped her to get through some of the tough times at home. Krystal is now going to college, double majoring in Genetics and Life Science Communications.

One spring and summer after her first year at college, Krystal signed up to be an intern for The College Works Program. It is a company that recruits college students to run their own business by painting houses. She spent many hours and miles going door to door to find houses to paint for the summer. Then she had to hire a couple of students to help her do the painting. Krystal is a petite young woman. She was carrying ladders and climbing on people's roofs. There were safety harnesses being used. This project took up her entire summer. It wasn't a money maker, but she gained a lot of personal growth with this project.

I was cleaning up in Krystal's room after she went back to college when I came upon a poem she had written. It greatly saddened me. It was written during that very hard time, when Kyle was in pain from the celiac disease, when his behaviors had become extremely irrational.

I think it's important for people to understand how hard it can be at times for the siblings of people with autism. Their feelings need validation. There are support groups for the parents, but I have never heard of any support groups for siblings. A sibling of a person who has autism or any disability has probably felt some animosity. It is not that they don't care about their sibling. They just need to vent and be heard.

With Krystal's consent, I have included her poem:

"The windows in my house used to all have locks

The doors in my house still do

And not just the ones that lead outside

But the closets and refrigerator too

Often, I struggle to find food and don't eat in my own living space

We all fear the ending consequences

If we leave the wrong food, in the wrong place

My family cannot do certain activities

And sometimes fear public eyes

A certain someone may have an episode

And scare those who stand by

I fear him too, whenever I hear, him

The frustration of his stomps and voice

He then does harmful acts, that I hide from

My parents do not get the same choice

He breaks things and tries to control things

If he can't control it, he breaks it

When it no longer works, he attacks

Every corner of the house can feel his fit

He'll try to dig his fingernails into something/often my mom

Sometimes my dad, sometimes my dogs

Who run into my room, and I try to keep them calm

I spend all my time in my room

But not even there, all is well

I don't see the sights

I hear every bang, every scream, every yell

Have you ever had reasonable resentment for someone?

But unable to place blame?

And if you ever expressed your feelings

Non-understanding faces, would look at you with shame

Because I can't explain in detail

The dark secrets of my life

So, they only think to accept those less fortunate

No matter the surrounding strife

How could they understand what it is like?

My brother has severely low-functioning autism

Which is further distressed by many dietary issues

Including stomach yeast, celiac disease, prediabetes

How could they understand?"

I believe Krystal had become afraid to come out to the kitchen to get something to eat. I was going through my own misery and didn't notice. At the time, I was just glad that she was safely tucked away in her room. But it must have been very frustrating for her.

I cannot convey how I felt when I read this. Krystal is always so quietly patient. I know how important it is to express how one is feeling, especially in times of stress. I'm glad she thought to write down how she felt. It does help. I wonder how many other siblings of autistic individuals are struggling the way Krystal was. Currently, Krystal is in college. The situation has also greatly improved for when she does come home. She can come out of her room without fear. But I think she is right. Sometimes the siblings get overlooked in these types of situations. I'm sure there will be some siblings out there that will feel a camaraderie with Krystal when they read this.

In many ways, Krystal is a reflection of myself, yet we are so different in the way we grew up. Because of her brother, she has had her pains living in our household. However, she has had the self-confidence to go out and find creative and healthy outlets for herself. I didn't have that self-confidence at her age. I went in a completely different direction.

Krystal didn't even know I had drinking problem in my earlier years. I mentioned it to her when I told her I was writing a book. She just knew that I didn't drink alcohol. Krystal does not drink alcohol.

Krystal is a vegetarian by choice. She will not eat anything that has a face! That is what she says. Krystal does not eat the same foods that Mike, Erik, and I eat, but there has always been food in the refrigerator for her to eat. The refrigerator has a combination lock. We all know the combination except for Kyle. One time, we tried putting a small refrigerator in Krystal's room. Kyle broke the lock on it. I had also bought her a case with a lock on it. It was something to hide her snacks in. But Kyle broke that too. He has not broken the lock on the refrigerator in the kitchen. However, at one point, he became very dexterous with using a screwdriver. He unscrewed the upper freezer door right off its hinges. He really wanted that ice cream in the ice box! We must now hide our tools too.

Like Kyle, Krystal received all her vaccinations when she was little. Erik did as well. But Erik was first, and they hadn't started increasing the vaccinations with the thimerosal yet. Krystal came after Kyle, but I still wasn't all that educated yet about the dangers of vaccinations. I was still believing that Kyle just had autism.

Being that Krystal seemed to do okay with receiving her vaccinations, I was at first okay with her receiving the HPV vaccination for cervical cancer. But she only received the first shot. There are three that you are supposed to get for the prevention of cervical cancer. A couple of days after receiving the shot, she had a terrible headache and asked me for a painkiller to get rid of it. This was extremely unusual. This was the one and only time in Krystal's life that she had ever asked for something to take for a headache. She had never done that before, and she never did it again. She wasn't having her menstrual cycle at the time. I had asked her.

I mentioned this to my friend who has a daughter the same age as Krystal. She reminded me of the dangers of the vaccines. I did some research and was appalled by how many girls have either died or become paralyzed by this vaccination. I have researched that it is not even that effective. There was no way I was going to bring Krystal in again for another shot. Some of these other girls had a headache after their first shot and then died after their second shot! One died after her first shot, but of course, it is denied that the vaccine was the cause. The book *The HPV Vaccine on Trial* is informative about this vaccine. It is written by Mary Holland, J.D., Kim Mack Rosenberg, J.D., and Eileen Iorio.

Erik and Krystal have both been involved in numerous activities while growing up, but not too involved in sports. My kids are not athletes, and neither was I. Mike tried wrestling and track in high school. He also liked downhill skiing. Erik tried cross country running in high school, but it wasn't for him. Krystal tried playing girls' basketball, but that wasn't for her either. I give them credit for trying.

Through the school system, Krystal participated in Debate, Forensics, Model UN, Mock Trials, Drama Troupe, and SEED. She was particularly involved in the Drama Club. She worked behind the scenes with the crew. After working on so many plays and musicals, she became the stage crew manager. Krystal continued to work on many more plays and musicals.

She also volunteered to work at a community drama theatre. Also, through the school system, Krystal has been to Washington D.C., and she spent a few weeks in Germany with her German class.

Many of Krystal's choices of extracurricular activities challenged her mind. Erik likes to challenge his mind too, but he does so in his accounting job and by playing strategic games. It is hard to beat Erik in a game! Mike and I do win occasionally, but Erik wins the majority of the time. During their school and college years, both Erik and Krystal were, and are, mostly straight A students!

When Krystal was younger, she was in dance classes for nine years. She was involved in Project SEEK for several years. This stands for, Services to Enable and Empower Kids. For this program, she received an award for "Consistently positive volunteering efforts in support of our local community and youth."

Erik was a member of the Boy Scouts of America during his years in elementary school. He won the Pine Derby Race one year. Erik played the baritone in band during middle school. He volunteered for numerous years at the equestrian center where Kyle rode horses. As an adult, he joined the Big Brothers, Big Sisters Organization. He has been a big brother to a boy for several years.

Erik enjoys his tech games, like so many young people do today. But he also enjoys swimming, biking, and cross-country skiing. He enjoys doing the Tough Mudder Challenge. It is an obstacle course through the mud.

One activity that I signed both Erik and Krystal up for when they were in middle school was Air Camp. They got a chance to steer an airplane with an instructor at their side. When Erik participated in the program, he got to go up in a helicopter. When Krystal participated, she got to ride in a glider plane. It was a good experience!

Both Erik and Krystal took swimming lessons at the YMCA for several years. They are both good swimmers.

Once, Erik went swimming around a lake with his grandmother. He was a young adult at the time, but I honestly wasn't thrilled about this. I was worried. He is a good swimmer, but still not as experienced as his grandmother was. Grandma wanted him to go with her.

My dad used to worry about my mother doing this long-distance swimming. He would paddle a canoe along the side of her when she went. No one was with Mom and Erik in a boat when they went.

My mother put a scenic design on her and my father's gravestone. On the gravestone, there is the camp (a log cabin) with wood animals, such as an eagle, deer, loons, and a raccoon. It is pictured on a lake (but the camp is not really on a lake). My dad is paddling the canoe along the side of my mom, who is swimming in the lake. It is quite beautiful, just as I would expect from my mother!

My parents' camp and the property were bought out from us by my sister's two sons. I'm sure my parents are pleased and smiling down on them for buying it, on the other side!

19
FURRY FAMILY MEMBERS & SEIZURES

In addition to my off-spring, I currently have four of the furry four-footed kind! My fabulous, furry, sensitive, Keeshond dog, Shadow, and cute, needy, nutty Cockapoo, Mulan. Plus, my sweet, slick, and smooth-looking, but troublemaking, Bengal cat (not tiger), Aries, and my beautifully soft, loyal, blue-eyed Birman cat, Loki. I had always had stray animals for my pets in the past, except for Skipper. I decided that my next pets were going to be purebreds. But Mulan is a half-breed.

Our current precious Keeshond dog, Shadow, has seizures. It is characteristic of his breed. Shadow typically has two seizures once per month. One day, he started having a cluster of seizures. He had seven that day. We brought him to the pet emergency room in our area. He stayed the night to get his seizures under control with valium. I have resisted putting him on seizure medication. I have read the medications can lead to liver and kidney problems down the road. I started giving him herbal calming supplements. It seemed to help for a while. Unfortunately, eight months after having the cluster of seizures, he had another cluster of seizures. I finally broke down and put him on the seizure medication, Keppra.

The first cluster of seizures started after Shadow had his annual vaccinations. I fear him getting any more of them. I had also noticed that he would have a seizure shortly after I gave him a heartworm pill. I will not give him any more of those. My other dog, Mulan, does fine with taking her heartworm pills and getting vaccinations. Our former dog, Gambit, did fine with them as well. But some dogs don't.

There are also other breeds that are more susceptible to seizures. My brother's Bulldog was also more prone, and he died having seizures.

Pets are an important part of the family too. All my children grew up with animals in the house. We had a half Golden Retriever mutt. He was our dog, Gambit. We had him for fifteen years. He had been more of Erik's dog. Then we also had the four other cats that I mentioned earlier.

Kyle has been fine with our pets through most of his years growing up with them. It was only when the celiac disease became so bad and he was in pain, that he became aggressive and started the pinching, that I had to worry about the dogs. The cats would hide, so he didn't bother them. He wasn't aggressive towards the dogs during the insanity period; he was mostly ignoring them at that time. We do, however, still need to give him reminders to pet gently. His petting can be a little intense sometimes.

We also had other pets. We have had an iguana, ferrets, a turtle, rabbit, guinea pig, and two parakeets. But not all at the same time!

Many people diagnosed with autism also suffer from seizures.

Kyle does not. We are fortunate. Kyle was tested for seizures when he was first diagnosed with autism. In most of the other families that I know who have a child with autism, the child also has seizures. I don't envy that they need to put their children on seizure medications. It is very hard to watch Shadow have a seizure. I cannot imagine what it is like to watch your child have one.

However, Kyle certainly does have his share of serious problems! I have wondered as to why Kyle does not have seizures too. I have read on Google that breastfeeding your children might be a deterrent from them having seizures. I don't know. I did breastfeed all three of my children. Erik for just a few months, but Kyle and Krystal I breastfed for nearly two years.

Erik's 3rd Birthday

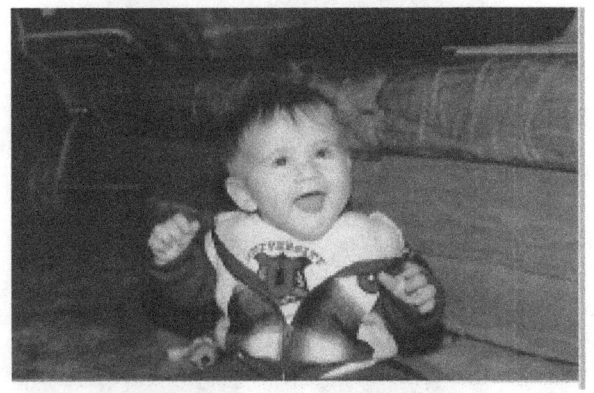

Kyle at about 6 months old, looking at camera

PHOTOS II

Erik & Kyle

Erik, Kyle, and Krystal

PHOTOS II

Kyle & Krystal/Kyle looking off

Krystal in Dance Recital Outfit

Kyle on Horse at Equestrian Therapy

PHOTOS II

Shadow & Mulan

Ares & Loki

PHOTOS II

Ares in Christmas Tree

20
HEALING ONESELF

After having a biopsy, I was told by my gynecologist that I had precancerous cells. To be more specific, I was told it was complex endometrial hyperplasia with atypia. It is a condition where a woman has an excess growth of cells in her uterus. Women with this condition are commonly found to have endometrial cancer while their hysterectomy is being performed. I had a full hysterectomy at 48 years old, in 2010. Absolutely everything was removed. This included the uterus, cervix, fallopian tubes, and ovaries.

After my surgery, I will always remember the gynecologic oncologist yelling out to me as I came out of the anesthetic, "NO CANCER." It was wonderful to hear!

A different doctor who came to check on me at the hospital afterwards said that he didn't think the oncologist should have told me that I had no cancer before the test results came back from the lab. But the oncologist knew his profession. The tests came back negative.

I had this paranoid feeling that they would tell me that I had cancer and would start shoving chemotherapy and radiation at me if it were not for the oncologist. I had good insurance. I'm grateful to him for giving me a head's up!

To this day, I'm not sure if I really needed that surgery. We all have precancerous cells. I do like the idea that those precancerous cells were taken out. But then again, they may not have ever turned into cancer.

After the surgery, I started having trouble with my right leg. I don't know what happened to it during that surgery. It must have been in the way during surgery. I had right hip problems, and the muscles in my right thigh would tighten up sometimes when I walked. I would have to stop and let the muscles loosen up again before I could walk again. It didn't do this before the surgery. Soon after the surgery, I made an appointment for an ultrasound for my leg. I was afraid I might have gotten blood clots from the surgery. This turned out to be negative. But I will always remember the look on the technician's face when she observed my ultrasound. Her expression was disturbing to me. She saw something that wasn't good in that ultrasound. I never did find out what was going on with my leg.

In my opinion, the reason my precancerous cells may not have turned into cancer was because of all the supplements I take. At the time of my surgery, I was taking green tea, reduced glutathione, garlic, MSM, milk thistle, probiotics, vitamins A, C & E Complex, and D3.

I have since added turmeric, glucosamine, cayenne garlic, calcium, holy basil, folic acid, saffron, essiac tea, gaba, DIM, echinacea, parsley and proteolytic enzymes. Yes, I'm a little obsessive about my supplements!

I'm a believer in naturopathy methods of healing your body. Many of the supplements have anti-inflammatory properties and contain lots of antioxidants.

Plus, I like to drink a lot of herbal tea. I like black, cinnamon, dandelion, hibiscus, and chamomile teas. They are full of antioxidants too. I like decaffeinated, because caffeine makes my head spin and can give me a headache.

I believe the supplements and teas help keep those precancerous cells from developing into full-blown cancer. I also like to snack on blueberries and raspberries. Lots of antioxidants!

Like many people, I have struggled with my weight for most of my life. I mentioned earlier that I had lost eighty pounds when I was younger. But after that, I had two more children, which put on some pounds. Plus, raising a child with autism has been stressful, and food became a subsequent addiction. I gained more weight when Kyle's behaviors became worse. I was still exercising at the Y regularly, but I wasn't watching what I ate. I was up to 276 pounds at 5'6" tall.

It was becoming hard for me to stand or walk. My injuries I sustained after my surgery made the issue even worse. I have read online accounts of other women complaining about hip and lower back problems after their hysterectomies. Some about leg problems too. My lower back and right hip hurt terribly after standing for just a short time. I had to lean on the grocery cart to go shopping. Once, I attempted to look at greeting cards after I finished putting my groceries in my cart, but I couldn't stand for much longer, even though I was leaning on a cart. I needed to check out and get back to my car. I felt like crying. It seemed like such a simple task. I wanted to cry because I knew I was going downhill. It was becoming routine for me to have to sit down and rest my aching body when I got back to my car, before putting the groceries in the car.

I preferred shopping online rather than going to a store. It was hard to walk into a store without a cart. I had to lean on Mike to just walk into a store. I was starting to know how my mother felt in her last years. But I was only in my fifties, not my seventies!

I used a bar stool in the kitchen to cook and do dishes. Mike took over the vacuuming. I was walking hunched over. I felt old, as if I was in my eighties or nineties. I could still walk the treadmill for maybe fifteen minutes, but that was only because I was holding on to the bars.

I also have had trouble with plantar fasciitis in my feet. I had that problem ten years before my back and hip problems. This is an inflammation of a thick band of tissue that connects the heel bone to the toes. It is extremely painful when you stand up in the morning, because you stretch that band that has shrunk up overnight.

I didn't like crawling down the hall to get to the bathroom in the night. This is what I had done when my plantar fasciitis first started acting up. I hadn't yet understood what was wrong with my foot, and I continued to do a lot of walking with it on the treadmill. It became very bad because of all the pressure I was putting on it.

First, it happened with my left foot. I started wearing a night splint to bed every night after the doctor explained to me what was wrong with it. I did that for about five years. I also started wearing orthotics in my shoes to help alleviate the pain.

The left foot started to heal, but then my right foot started to go bad. The night splint didn't seem to be working on that foot. Instead, I found a wrap from King Brand products on Amazon. They also have their own website. The wrap has really helped my foot. In addition, if I start feeling my feet ache again after overdoing exercise, I wear a night splint too. King Brand also has wraps for many different parts of your body. I have one to put on my right thigh, the leg that bothered me after the hysterectomy. It has helped. The wrap operates by "blood flow stimulation therapy." It helps your body heal itself.

I found another magnificent device on Amazon that has helped my back and hips. It is a Far Infrared Amethyst Mat. I call it my magic mat. It includes negative ions, red photon lights, and PEMF (Pulsed Electromagnetic Field).

As stated on WebMD, "Negative Ions create positive vibes... Negative Ions are odorless, tasteless, and invisible molecules that we inhale in abundance in certain environments. Think mountains, waterfalls and beaches. Negative ions neutralize free radicals."

Red Photon Light Therapy is also said to be very beneficial for your health.

According to umich.edu, "The four elements of western culture are: EARTH, AIR, FIRE, and WATER. These four elements were believed to be essential to life." As most of us know, living things on Earth need food, water, oxygen, and sunlight to survive. Our bodies need nutrients from our food, oxygen to breathe, and we need to hydrate with water.

The author Andreas Moritz has written numerous books on alternative health. He wrote one book called, *Healing with Sunlight*, regarding our health needs for sunlight. He also wrote about the chemical poisons in sunscreen in this book. He suggests sunscreen can cause cancer. But yes, too much sun on the skin can be damaging too.

PEMF (Pulsed Electromagnetic Field) has many health benefits. Our bodies need the PEMF element, in addition to the other elements. It comes from the Earth's geomagnetic field. In today's world, many of us spend too much time inside with our modern devices that give out electromagnetic smog. It is making us sick.

We came from the earth. We are a part of it. We need to be spending more time outdoors to receive its benefits. But in the winter months in the Midwest, that is hard to do.

If you are interested in knowing more, I would suggest reading *PEMF, The Fifth Element of Earth* by Bryant A. Meyers. The book is a wonder! There is no other like it. Bestselling author Ty M. Bollinger also has a segment about PEMF in his book *The Truth about Cancer*. I highly recommend his books. Another book of his I recommend is *Monumental Myths of the Modern Medical Mafia and Mainstream Media and the Multitude of Lying Liars that Manufactured Them*. His books are educational, and he explains how the FDA and Big Pharma all began. Vaccines are not the only poison people are being given. There are alternative treatments for cancer. Our bodies can heal themselves if we take care of them properly. Another interesting book is *The Paleo Cardiologist: The Natural Way to Heart Health*, written by Jack Wolfson DO, FACC. He talks about the myths about cholesterol.

After using my Far Infrared Amethyst Mat for only a couple of months, I started feeling the benefits. I believe the PEMF is the most beneficial part of the device, but the other benefits are very important as well. It infuses the cells in your body with energy. It soothes your aches and pains. It has helped my hip and back. I can now grocery shop standing straight, and not hunched over the cart. I don't even need the support of a cart to walk around a store anymore.

On the Far Infrared Mat, there is a heat setting. You can use a high heat setting and be on the mat for a short period of time, or you can set it to a low heat setting and sleep on the mat all night. I choose to sleep on it all night on a lower heat setting. I cannot say it is as comfortable as a mattress, but is fine and you get used to it. You just might feel that you need to turn over a little more during the night, but it is well worth it for how it makes me feel the next day!

Not only are my aches and pains diminishing, but I'm not as tired. It has given me energy. I used to have to take an afternoon nap every day or I couldn't get through a whole day. I couldn't drive a long distance because I would feel myself start to nod off. It is rare for me to take a nap anymore. I can also drive longer distances now.

The Amethyst Mat may have even helped me lose weight. I have used the treadmill for many years, and I didn't lose weight. But now I was able to. I had also started dieting. I'm sure that losing the weight further aided in relieving my aches and pains. It is a slow process. I lost weight at about two pounds per week. It has taken over a year, but I have lost about 80 pounds and still counting. Losing weight does make you feel like a new person.

Something else that I take at night is Boswellia Frankincense, ginger and cinnamon. They are all anti-inflammatory. I alternate between them. I believe my right thigh developed arthritis in it from the injury. It does not tighten up anymore after having used the Amethyst Mat and the King Brand wraps. But despite the improvements, it can still ache during the night, especially when I'm not sleeping with that side on my mat. These supplements help to alleviate the pain. Willow Bark helps as well. I prefer the more natural painkillers. Occasionally, I will bring myself to take an ibuprofen if it is too bothersome during the night. But not often.

During the day when I'm moving around and the blood is circulating, I have no further issues with my lower back and right hip. They don't hurt at all anymore. The mat combined with weight loss has completely helped to heal that issue. I no longer need to use a chair in my kitchen to cook or do the dishes. I no longer need a cart for support while shopping.

After using the mat for just a month or two, I was already getting relief from my back and hip pains, and I also had more energy. I wish I'd known about these devices when my mother was still alive, but I don't know if she would have been willing to try them.

My diet includes eating the same food every weekday. In the morning, I eat a little Salisbury meat with gravy from a favorite TV dinner that I like. I throw away the potatoes from it every day. I like to put my Himalayan salt on it. I will only buy Himalayan salt. It is healthier with all the natural minerals in it. It is better for your heart than table salt. Celtic Sea salt is good too. This part of my meal is my salt fix for the day. However, you still shouldn't consume large amounts of salt of any kind.

Another part of my diet is to eat a big salad. It contains organic lettuce, a few spicy hemp seeds, a few bacon bits, and just a little shredded sharp cheddar cheese. I used a fat-free Italian vinegar dressing. I also eat a very tiny cup of ice cream topped with toffee chips. I love my toffee. But when it comes to food, nothing is worse for the body than sugar. Sugar feeds cancer cells, causes inflammation, triggers acne, and makes you fat. But I love the taste of it as much as the next person! I have just learned not to eat so much of it. Lastly on my diet, I have a Nutrisystem turbo chocolate shake both in the morning and at dinner time. This is all I have for dinner. Then in the evening, I snack on blueberries or raspberries.

On the weekends, I go off the diet, but I still make sure that I don't eat so much that I gain weight back. That is the tricky part! I do some calorie counting. We get take-out food on the weekends. You can find out the number of calories of fast food places online. I always look forward to that food on the weekends, but then I'm ready to go back to the strict diet on Monday. This is how I lose weight. I think that walking the treadmill or striding on the elliptical is very beneficial when combined with the diet. Recently, I've been preferring the elliptical to the treadmill because it is easier on my feet. It is also more of a full-body workout!

In the summer, I like to ride my bike on a trail along the river. I don't do it every day because my left knee can bother me while doing this. A Pit Bull rammed into my knee at a dog park we went to. The owner saw me wail out in pain, but she just turned her back and walked away. I don't care to bring my dogs to dog parks anymore. Thankfully, my knee does not bother me at any other time.

There have been other maladies in our family to be very concerned about. One family member had an emergency appendix removal. He was having a lot of pain, so he went to see a doctor. They had tests taken, and he was immediately admitted into the hospital to have surgery. He was very lucky that his appendix hadn't burst. It was serious. This family member had recently had a colonoscopy. He asked his doctor if that could have had anything to do with it. He was given the impression that the doctor felt it was because of the colonoscopy. Having a colonoscopy nearly led to his death.

My mother would never have a colonoscopy or even a mammogram. She knew someone who had had a colonoscopy and ended up having to eat with a feeding tube the rest of her life. I will never have a colonoscopy. I will not have mammograms anymore either. I do realize that there are people who benefit, especially people who have a history of colon cancer in their families. It should be left up to an individual what risks one should or shouldn't take. They shouldn't be pressured into it by a doctor. I don't believe in preventative medical procedures. It is mostly a money-making scheme as far as I'm concerned. That is how I feel about it. I have read that these so-called preventive tests are more damaging to our bodies than helpful. Mammograms squish our tissue in our breasts. The X-ray part of it increases your chance of getting breast cancer after having them for numerous years.

As I stated earlier, I still believe doctors are very important. We need emergency rooms, surgeons, and more. When Krystal was three years old, I noticed that she didn't seem to be able to keep up with her friend and she had temper tantrums. I started to wonder if I had another child with autism. At the pediatrician's office, a heart murmur was detected. We were recommended to take her to a cardiologist. It turned out that she had an atrial septal defect. This means that she had a hole in her heart. She was only three years old, and the hole in her heart was the size of a quarter!

Krystal had to have open-heart surgery. I cannot tell you how terrifying that was for us. I finally had my baby girl, and now I was so afraid I would lose her. But if we hadn't had the surgery, her heart would have become enlarged. This could have resulted in a short life span for her. Krystal had heart surgery, and she has done very well ever since. I appreciate all the doctors that participated in making her well, including our primary pediatrician!

EPILOGUE | PART 1

Regarding my siblings, I talk on the phone periodically to my brother. We have some nice long conversations. I text with my sister sometimes, and we exchange greeting cards for holidays and birthdays. This was something my mother had liked to do. Both my sister and I inherited the holiday greeting card bug, along with the decorating bug. My sister and I also occasionally talk on the phone.

After my mother's passing, my siblings and I went through all my mother's photos. It took us several days. It was nice feeling to have the three of us together to reminisce. But there was one item that we came across that was a bit disturbing to me. It was one of my mother's old wallets. It contained numerous photos, including some my brother, sister, and numerous others. But there was no photo of me. I looked at the date on one of the items. It indicated that she was using this wallet when I was around eighteen years old. This would have been during my early years of alcoholism. My guess is that she wasn't pleased with me at that time. I didn't

EPILOGUE | PART 1

want the wallet. I gave it to my sister, but I didn't say anything about what I was thinking.

I don't know if my brother and sister will agree with everything I have expressed about our family, particularly our mother. But based on my experiences, it makes sense to me!

I saw the twins at my mother's funeral visitation. It had been many years since I had seen them. I was ecstatically happy to see Mandy and Sandy. It had been about ten years since I had seen Mandy, and nearly thirty years since I had seen Sandy. I just hugged them and told them that I loved them. They said they loved me back. These girls had been more than friends to me. They had helped to sustain me during a time when I was losing myself. I don't know what I would done without their friendship. Their bubbly personalities have a way of taking me away from the grimness of life!

I finally was able to get together with Mandy and Sandy when I went up north to go through the photographs with my siblings. It was wonderful just having lunch and doing a little shopping with them. It had always been hard to get together with them when my entire family went up to visit my mother, mostly because of Kyle. It took multiple eyes to keep an eye on him. After Mom passed away, I decided that I would go visit up north on my own. Mike stayed home with Kyle. I did the same for him, when he attended his 30-year school reunion out of state.

My mother spent her final days at a nursing home. My sister and I felt that the nursing home had given mom more medication than she could handle, even if it wasn't considered an unusual amount. It was too much for my mother. Mom was sensitive to medications. When she had been at the Green Bay Hospital, she had still been doing okay. She was still speaking fine at that time. Then she had to move into a nursing home. Then it was only a couple of days before she had her cardiac arrest.

At the nursing home, there were times when she could barely even speak. The last time I spoke to her on the phone while she at the nursing home, all she could say was, "Ah, ah." I said "I love you" one last time. My sister was holding the phone for her. It would be the last time I spoke to her.

I called the nursing home on the morning that Mom died. I attempted to talk to someone about how I felt her medications were affecting her. I left a message with the receptionist. When I got a phone call from them that afternoon, I thought they were calling me back, but they were calling to tell me that my mother had passed.

I don't how much longer my mother could have hung on, despite too much medication. She was in a dire condition. Her life would have been very painful and a huge struggle if she had lived longer. My mother seemed to know that she wasn't going to make it.

I will always love my mother. In later years, I felt we had grown to have a special relationship. She seemed to intuitively know when I was going to call her. I'm still saddened by her death.

But after her death, I was free to admit to myself that she may have failed to give me the emotional support that I needed. Our relationship had a rough start, with her being hospitalized for that skin condition that was caused from her nerves when I was just a baby.

But it is more than that. I believe my mother had somewhat of a mean-spirited streak. I believe she was a covert narcissist.

I saw this behavior displayed not only toward myself, but toward others as well.

My mother had this ability to display this wonderful personality to the world. She also had an uncanny ability to accomplish and achieve whatever she set her mind to. My mother displayed many acts of kindness to those around her. I learned politeness from my mother. She was a fabulous grandmother. All her grandchildren adored her.

It may have been an accumulation of circumstances as to why I grew up with such low self-esteem that led me to suffer from chronic alcoholism. But in my opinion, the covert narcissism characteristic seems to fit the bill where my mother is concerned. I have come to accept that was just who she was. I can forgive her. I never feared her while growing up. In my adult years, we got along wonderfully! I was oblivious to her being anything but a great mom! The mind is a powerful thing! I believed what I needed to, growing up, in order to survive. Sometimes I did fear my dad's temper. He could be loud. But I always knew deep down that he had my back and would do anything for me! I learned integrity from my father.

I no longer want to stuff my feelings as I did when I was a child. I was asked by a friend if writing down my experiences about Kyle was cathartic. I have had a lot of hard struggles in raising Kyle, and I have shed tears. But I also have always had people to talk to, including my husband, my family, and my good friends, Lynn and Debbie. Plus, yes, there was also my mother! There are no repressed memories where Kyle is concerned. No secrets.

I did experience catharsis when writing about my early years and my alcoholism. My secrets! Those memories were my stuffed feelings.

I was on my way to dying from alcoholism. There was an underlying reason why I felt so poorly about myself. I didn't have solid memories to explain it. I could never really figure it out. I even went so far as to wonder if I carried some deep grief from a prior life.

But we come with a clean slate when we are reincarnated. Otherwise, we would have nothing to learn. We forget our grievances. I do believe that some of our inner characteristics from our former selves may come through into our new lives. But we develop new personalities based on our environment and upbringing. That is what I believe.

I'm sure my mother never intended for me to become an alcoholic. I don't believe that is what she really wanted for me.

It took my dad 48 years to see beneath the surface of who my mother really was. My dad deserves justice for whatever it was he was trying to tell me, "Your mother, she is not as she seems." I also deserve justice. My sister as well. I believe my brother was the least affected in an unfavorable way by my mother.

I believe my mother raised her children the best that she knew how. I also think she tried to be a good person during her time on this earth. It was just in her innate character to be somewhat spiteful now and then. It was as if she couldn't help herself! At her core, she could be a bit ill-natured at times. She lacked empathy. Despite her shortcomings, I believe she really did love all three of her children, and my father. Plus, certainly her grandchildren!

EPILOGUE | PART 2

In my married life family, we are very relieved that we can live life fairly, normal once again where Kyle is concerned—at least, what we consider to be normal. We still feel that we should keep the doors locked with a bolt. However, we don't always use the locks on the windows anymore. We are still limited to places we would like to visit or restaurants we would like to go to. When Mike takes a day off from work, we like to go out to eat for lunch while Kyle is at his day service program. It is enjoyable.

When Erik was twelve years old and Kyle was four years old, we took a vacation to South Dakota to visit Mount Rushmore and the Badlands. Krystal was born the following year. I remember doing a lot of chasing after Kyle during that vacation. We would only go to take-out restaurants because Kyle would climb over the booth to where people were sitting on the other side.

Other vacations that we went were to the Wisconsin Dells, which was nearby. It is always a nice place to visit. Our whole family, except for Kyle, did some zip-lining one year! Kyle did enjoy the jet boats with us. He was doing a lot of smiling! Krystal was a teenager by this time, and the boys were young adults.

In addition, not long ago, we had gone on a vacation and stayed in a luxurious cabin on a beautiful lake. Plus, we had a fun, scenic ride on a pontoon boat to see the magnificent Pictured Rocks on Lake Superior in the Upper Peninsula. Again, Kyle really enjoyed the boat ride!

These trips were all times to remember! Mike and I have a goal to see the Grand Canyon and the Colorado Mountains before we pass on. Recently, Mike and I attended a Pat Benetar and Neil Giraldo concert at the *Gathering on the Green* in Wisconsin. It was an outdoor event. We had good seats in the third row. This is something unusual for us to do. Erik volunteered to babysit Kyle. I just love Pat Benetar's powerful voice! I think it empowers women. It makes me feel that way.

It could have just been my imagination, but I could have sworn that Pat and Neil glanced over our way. I was wearing my cute fashionable cowgirl hat because of the bright sunshine earlier in the day when we were listening to the local bands before the main concert.

One of Kyle's favorite nearby places to visit is the Milwaukee Zoo. Our family visited there annually for many years. Kyle still visits the zoo periodically with his day service program. Kyle has always been fond of the animals. His favorites are the hippopotamus, elephant, and rhinoceros. He seems to like those big, bulky, fantastic creatures!

Presently at home, Kyle enjoys looking at YouTube videos on his iPad. I try to find the videos that are child safe. He likes the silly ones. He also likes his LeapFrog Android-based Kids Tablet. I think he likes the tablets because he has control of the device. Kyle does not have much control over his own life. It is one of the sad realities of low-functioning autism.

We continue to live one day a time. We are always hoping and praying for any type of improvement. There are some days where he seems to feel okay in his body. But his behavior is still inconsistent and can vary from day to day, depending on his digestion or sensory issues. I'm always worried about the day that I won't be here anymore to protect and care for him. It is so incredibly easy to give him something that throws off his entire system.

Kyle's struggles have been difficult to deal with, but the thought of abandoning him tears at the core of my soul. If anyone deserves justice, it is my son Kyle, and the many others like him. Along with their families. I hope that in telling Kyle's story, it might help others and that his suffering will not be in vain. It is scary to think where our world is going in regard to vaccines. Autism is more from environmental causes, not genetic. When Kyle has these extreme reactions to small amounts of toxins in his system, it tells me that his condition has been affected by environmental factors. We wouldn't be having this rapid increase if it was just genetic. That seems like logic to me.

I find it interesting that you continuously hear about people dying from the flu, without any detailed information on their prior health. But it is a rare occasion that you hear about the individual tragic stories of parents and their children with autism. You only hear about how much autism has skyrocketed. The number of vaccines being given increased during the time thimerosal was wholly being used in them.

(Isn't that a coincidence that autism increased at the same time!)

If this autism epidemic continues, everyone will know of someone who has autism. Who will take care of these individuals? Who will love them? These agencies who are responsible for distributing the toxic vaccines are more interested in money and wealth. If I sound angry, I am! I have a right to be! This autism epidemic is bringing the mama bear out of many mothers! The papa bears too!

The same goes for the tragic stories of the parents and their children who were vaccinated with the HPV vaccine, Gardasil. Thanks to the Internet, some people are putting their stories online, but you don't hear much about these stories elsewhere. The mainline media always seems to defend vaccines.

People can sometimes be judgmental of parents of autistic individuals. They don't understand our day-to-day frustrations. We are not perfect. We make mistakes. But we love our afflicted children and are doing the best that we know how. The medical and mental health communities are not much help because they don't understand our children either. How can they when there is so much confusion about what is wrong with them! Parents are not believed about what is wrong with their children. We know there is more to it than what the medical community tells us. We parents all seem to be on the same page, and there are so many of us now. That cannot be just a coincidence. I know that I'm not alone in how I feel about vaccines and their connection with autism.

When I started my memoir, it was very cleansing to put my troubled early years on paper and get it out of my system. Something in my blood was boiling, and I needed to get it out! I continued writing about my life raising a child with autism, or in my eyes, his poisoning! I started to feel that it was important for people to hear about a family who has had to live with a child with autism. Even though, at first, I struggled to write about Kyle. But then all my feelings regarding his difficult life and our troubles started to pour out of me.

Some people may not approve of a parent writing about their child with autism. Some individuals who have autism can tell their own story, either verbally or through writing. They might say that it isn't a parent's story to tell. These individuals would be higher functioning than my son. He does not communicate. Kyle cannot read or write, and will never be able to. He is also very limited in what he understands. Kyle knows nothing of deceit, greed, or war.

In our state of Wisconsin, we have what is called a Wispact Trust set up for Kyle. The money put into it provides for the special needs of persons with disabilities without endangering their eligibility for public benefits, by making distributions to buy goods and services for the individual. Erik will be his guardian after Mike and I pass on. He will be able to do this for Kyle.

I would greatly disagree that Kyle's life's struggles are not mine to tell. When I have had bruises all over my arms, when I have been controlled, had my property destroyed, and when my life in general is restricted. It is very much about my life. It is our family's story. Krystal didn't think she could talk about how she was feeling, being cooped up in her room to avoid her brother. She didn't know how people would perceive her if she vented negative feelings about her brother, so she wrote it down. Kyle is the main victim in this situation, and we know that. We love him. We fight for him. But we are victims as well. I feel very strongly about not giving up on him, despite some very hard times I have endured. We are all survivors!

I wrote about Kyle to hopefully help educate people who are not familiar with low-functioning autism. I wrote about him to warn people about what I believe caused his condition. Most importantly, I wrote to protect him for the future when I'm gone or not in good health. I don't want future caregivers to repeat treatments that didn't work and made his condition worse. Other people don't have the many years of experience of intuitively reading his gestures. Kyle would be the one to suffer. I become very upset at the thought of people giving him the wrong food or giving him medications or supplements that he cannot tolerate. I will not be around forever, and his siblings don't understand everything about their brother. Erik will be his guardian (overseer) after we are gone, but he will not be his caretaker. Erik wouldn't be able to explain Kyle's issues. Mike doesn't understand everything about Kyle either. I have written down other detailed information to help with his care after I'm gone. I'm not planning on going anytime soon, but you never know what can happen, at any time.

Writing about Kyle's affliction and how it affects our family down on paper was stressful for me. It wasn't cathartic. However, the thought of sharing this information is cathartic for me. I feel that it's important for people to understand our awkward situation of dealing with autism, through my eyes. Through the eyes of a mother. The parents of people with autism know and understand their children better than anyone else.

I also wanted to be able to recommend the literature that I've come across. Literature that was written by people who have really done their homework! Helping to spread this news is the only way I know how to get justice for Kyle and others like him!

In my memoir, I started to wonder if I really wanted to put myself out there about my own personal hardships growing up. At the core, I'm still a very private person and I can still get emotional at times. I do still enjoy my time to myself, but I also very much enjoy chit-chatting away with friends. I'm not shy anymore.

I considered taking my early troubles out of the memoir and only writing about Kyle, even though that wasn't my intention when I began. I decided to leave in my early hardships in my book because they make me human. I'm fallible just like anyone else. Maybe more people can relate to me.

I will also have my story left behind after I'm gone, as I wanted. But I have more to do in this life. I'm needed. I hope that I will be around for a long time!

www.ingramcontent.com/pod-product-compliance
Lightning Source LLC
Chambersburg PA
CBHW061431040426
42450CB00007B/1000